THE APOSTOLIC CONGREGATION

THE APOSTOLIC CONGREGATION

Church Growth Reconceived for a New Generation

GEORGE G. HUNTER III

Abingdon Press
Nashville

THE APOSTOLIC CONGREGATION
CHURCH GROWTH RECONCEIVED FOR A NEW GENERATION

This book is printed on acid-free paper.

Library of Congress Cataloging-in-Publication Data

Hunter, George G., 1938-
    The apostolic congregation : church growth reconceived for a new generation / George G. Hunter III.
        p. cm.
    Includes bibliographical references.
    ISBN 978-1-4267-0211-2 (pbk : alk. paper)
1. Church Growth.   I. Title.
    BV652.2.H837 2009
    254'.5—dc22

2009016481

09 10 11 12 13 14 15 16 17 18—10 9 8 7 6 5 4 3 2 1

MANUFACTURED IN THE UNITED STATES OF AMERICA

To the memory of Bruce Larson,

reflective leader in church renewal,

who anticipated and dramatized

the renewal of apostolic vision

and suggested many of the strategic

themes now developed in this book

CONTENTS

FOREWORD

Gary L. McIntosh

My first encounter with George G. Hunter, III, was in 1980. He was a speaker at the Advanced Church Growth conference sponsored by the Institute for American Church Growth, which was held at the Hilton Hotel in Pasadena, California. My recollections of Dr. Hunter from that conference are that he was an astute observer of North American evangelism and church growth, as well as an articulate spokesperson for the Church Growth Movement.

Over the nearly thirty years since that first encounter, I have heard Dr. Hunter speak yearly at the annual meeting of the American Society for Church Growth, as well as in numerous other venues. My early impressions of him have been confirmed over and over. In my memory he is the only person to have spoken at every meeting of the Society, a tribute to his ability to capture the interest of the attendees on a regular basis. To the members of the American Society for Church Growth, his reputation for creative and precise expression of ideas is legendary, and he never disappoints.

By any responsible estimate, Dr. Hunter is one of the top two or three spokespersons for evangelism and church growth in the United States today. I say this for several reasons. First, Dr. Hunter understands his subject. He has been an observer of evangelism and church growth since the 1960s. In addition, he is one of just a handful of persons to have observed and analyzed the application of Donald McGavran's Church Growth missiology to North America from its modern beginnings in the 1970s to the postmodern present.

He writes from a thorough knowledge of his sources. While others have written about one narrow aspect of church growth (say, assimilation of newcomers or management of staff or allocation of resources), he has surveyed the entire landscape of Church Growth and has brought together a fresh study based on the whole body of literature available. What is impressive, however, is not only Dr. Hunter's knowledge of Church Growth literature but also his wide acquaintance with other fields of research. His application of insights from communication theory, history, ethics, theology, spiritual formation, and rhetoric, to name just a few fields, is impressive. I know of no other writer addressing evangelism and church growth who so ably integrates such a wide array of reading into his research.

Dr. Hunter is no "desk" theoretician! He is a "participant" observer and practitioner. Beginning with attempts to evangelize weight lifters at Muscle Beach in the 1960s, to visits with churches growing through conversion of secular peoples, to immersion in the Inuit Christian movement in Northern Canada, he engages church growth in the field, not simply in the library or study.

In *The Apostolic Congregation: Church Growth Reconceived for a New Generation*, Dr. Hunter restates core Church Growth principles and insights, but he also extends the categories and enlarges the knowledge about conversion evangelism beyond what is already known. In short, he plows new ground, revealing recent wisdom that helps churches be more fruitful in making disciples. His original ideas about catalytic growth, proliferation growth, movemental growth, and apostolic growth increase our understanding of how churches grow in today's complex environment.

From my perspective, this is a book that every serious student of evangelism and church growth must read. It not only explains in clear fashion what Church Growth really means, but it also points to apostolic Christianity's main business—making disciples of the nations for Jesus Christ.

Gary L. McIntosh, D.Min., Ph.D.
Professor, Christian Ministry & Leadership
Talbot School of Theology, Biola University
La Mirada, CA
March 2009

PREFACE

I grew up in the 1950s in Miami, Florida, as a fairly secular pagan. I say "fairly" secular because my family warmed to the religiosity of *Reader's Digest* and the Eisenhower era, which we mistook for Christianity. At some point, my mother taught me the Ten Commandments and the Lord's Prayer, and we attended a Presbyterian church "regularly" (as in annually), so we knew the name of the church we stayed away from 98 percent of the time. Sometimes I tried to pray, but I mainly viewed cosmic matters as a Deist; the Architect was far away. Several friends, notably Teddy Hubert, shared some of Christianity's message with me. I visited churches with him and others, and we had conversations. But the penny did not drop, the bell did not ring, and I did not yet discover the gift of faith.

In the summer of 1955, before my senior year in high school, I attended the international Key Club convention at the old Statler Hilton Hotel in Detroit. One evening, for our program, an actor named Gregory Wolcott, bearded and dressed in first-century Galilean attire, delivered the Sermon on the Mount—in the original King James English! At some point past the Beatitudes, I sensed the presence of God; I knew I was being approached and my name was being called. I knew that this presence was the God that Teddy and other friends had talked about, the God who gave his law in the commandments, to whom the Lord's Prayer is addressed. After the program, the presence followed me back to my room. In the Gideon Bible, I managed to find the Sermon on the Mount. I fell asleep reading and rereading it, aware for the first time that God is not the absentee landlord of Deism; the transcendent God was closer than I had ever imagined.

I awakened the next morning as the most aggressive "seeker" I have ever met. At breakfast, I questioned several fellows who were known to be Christians. One recommended a book, *Man Does Not Stand Alone*, by A. Cressy Morrison, a scientist. I bought it at a bookstore and read it between sessions. When I returned home, I visited the five churches in our community. Four churches were not interested in me— two because they were not interested in anyone who wasn't already a member, the other two because my reputation had preceded me.

The Fulford Methodist Church, however, welcomed me as though I had wandered into my true home for the first time. I discovered that I was more wanted at Fulford than anywhere else, and that the people there believed in me more than I believed in myself. Pastor Orville Nelson befriended me. He recommended books by E. Stanley Jones, and Jones's books connected me to John Wesley—theologian and apostle; my roots have been deeply planted in Wesley's tradition ever since. Nelson, Jones, and Wesley all insisted that I get into the Scriptures, so I did. I also visited Youth for Christ meetings, led by Ray Stanford. One night Stanford gave me a sheet of Bible verses to memorize, such as John 3:3 and 3:16, Ephesians 2:8-9, and the verses in Romans that were featured in the Roman Road. I learned them all by heart, and I discovered that the more Scripture I knew more or less by heart, the more Scripture was shaping my internal conversation.

In November of 1955, I experienced saving grace, believed, and committed my life to follow Jesus Christ as Lord. I experienced remarkable change in several areas of my life—change that was obvious to other people, including my parents, George and Barbara Hunter. People at Fulford Church visited Mom and Dad, and affirmed their son, and invited them to Fulford. They began attending. That winter, they too confessed faith and soon they invited another couple; and several of my friends became involved, and several of their friends, and so on. Our youth group doubled. The church was receiving new members by confession of faith month after month.

Fulford Methodist Church had its fair share of shortcomings, but the most important thing I took with me to college the next year was my church's quiet understanding of its main business. Although the church engaged in many ministries and activities, helping (what I now call) "pre-Christian" people find faith and a new life was top priority. When I later read the line from William Temple, "The True Church is the only society on earth that exists for its nonmembers," I realized that I had been "birthed" for a second time in a true church. I had been led to an apostolic congregation that knew a church is "sent out" by Christ to reach people like me.

◆　　　◆　　　◆　　　◆

In the next twenty years as I visited and worked in churches through college, divinity school, pastoral ministry, graduate school, and entrance into the teaching academy, I was astonished to find that only a minority of churches shared the priority of the church in which I'd found faith. Indeed, many church leaders were suspicious of churches that invited people who "weren't even Christians!" What such churches were doing, they said, was not "normal Christianity." By the 1970s, I heard that churches like Fulford offered "cheap grace" and that their members did not have "depth."

For all I knew, maybe the detractors were right; some of them were dedicated and educated, and they spoke with certitude. So I observed in many churches and, with a journalism background, interviewed people who regarded their view of Christianity as "normal." What I learned was seldom explicit; I had to read between the lines. But these were usually the driving assumptions: to be a Christian was, basically, to accept Jesus as your Savior so you could go to heaven when you died and, between now and then, you attended church, had a daily devotion, lived a "clean life," and participated in fellowship with other Christians. The local church's main business was to nurture its members, maintain its tradition, support the denomination, and support resolutions for civil rights. The "normal" churches did occasionally receive new members—who, from what I could tell, were already much like "good church people"! (I later made the connection that they were somewhat like the earliest church in Jerusalem, which only welcomed circumcised Gentiles!)

While I too believed in ministry to Christians, respect for tradition, and support for civil rights, what passed for "normal" Christianity seemed to be a domesticated form of "the faith once delivered to the saints," with some of the heart, more of the brain, and most of the vertebrae removed. That diluted version of Christianity would never change the world and would not have reached me. Perhaps my first church understood "the unsearchable riches of Christ" with more clarity and power than the "normal" churches!

◆   ◆   ◆   ◆

An immersion experience in the summer of 1962 ratified this conclusion. While still a divinity school student, I was assigned to ministry with the people of the Muscle Beach area of Santa Monica, California. Every day, Muscle Beach hosted the most heterogeneous population I have ever seen: the muscle crowd, beatniks, gays and lesbians, prostitutes, addicts, pushers, gamblers, criminals, sunbathers, surfers, roller skaters, shopkeepers, and others—including people speaking several languages. These affinity groups essentially coexisted on the same turf, with little communication between groups; for instance, the muscle crowd and the beatniks seldom fraternized. Furthermore, every group thought of itself as "different" from the others.

Nevertheless, virtually all of these people had one thing in common. They had no idea what I was talking about! They were more secular than I had been in my "BC" life in Miami. They had no serious Christian background, no Christian memory; most did not know or even recognize the Lord's Prayer and many could not tell me the name of the church that they, their parents, or their grandparents stayed away from.

My background in secularity enabled me to identify with them. They taught me to begin where they were and to communicate in their language, not in the church's language. I became deeply convinced that, although many of them were not at all like "good church people," they nevertheless mattered to God and therefore ought to matter to the church. About a dozen people became believers that summer and, as fishermen say, I "influenced" others.

I experienced firsthand their contrasting perceptions of Jesus Christ and his church. They were interested in Jesus. They were open to what Jesus taught, to what we believe about him, and to what it means to follow him.

They were remarkably less interested in Christ's church. Many of Muscle Beach's people who'd never been inside a church had heard that churches are "boring," and "irrelevant," and "not interested in people like us." Even those who discovered faith were reluctant to go with me to church. No one who went with me once would agree to go again. Although no church stopped anyone from attending, my friends were astute readers of body language; they sensed that the people either didn't care about them or were suspicious of them and, in any case, they experienced church as almost as boring and irrelevant as their grapevine had said. In that period, I was dealing with more questions and issues than I could cope with, but two things were obvious to me. It did not seem that any church's priority was engaging people like my friends, and the churches assumed that the way they did church was "normal" Christianity.

I never got over the summer of 1962. I soon perceived that the number of secular people was growing in *all* of our communities, that our communities were become mission fields—something like what had already occurred in most of Western Europe—and most of our churches were sleeping through this demographic revolution. I read books on evangelism and mission. I did a PhD in Communication Studies at Northwestern University and discovered that the communication of Christianity's message to people who have little or no prior familiarity with it is an even more complex challenge than I had imagined. I interviewed more and more secular people, and (especially) converts from secularity. I began the long-term task of studying the occasional Christian advocates and churches that were reaching pre-Christian people.

◆　　　◆　　　◆　　　◆

One day in 1973, while teaching evangelism at the Perkins School of Theology at Southern Methodist University, I received a book in the mail that was to accelerate my learning curve. Win Arn had interviewed Donald McGavran at great length, edited the transcripts, and published *How To Grow a Church*. I read it over the course of the next two evenings. McGavran was dean emeritus of Fuller Theological Seminary's School of World Mission. He had spent a lifetime asking questions much like mine, and the range and depth of his understanding was light-years ahead of mine. The bibliography featured eight more books to read, including the first edition of McGavran's *Understanding Church Growth*. I ordered and read those books and others, and then spent a sabbatical with McGavran in 1977. I was hooked. I have functioned ever since with one foot in the Church Growth school of thought and with the other foot in the broader communication, ministry, and apostolic concerns that have gripped me all along.

In time, I wrote books from the Church Growth perspective. *To Spread the Power: Church Growth in the Wesleyan Spirit* (Abingdon Press, 1987) interpreted the insights for mainline church leaders and demonstrated that some of McGavran's discoveries were rediscoveries; John Wesley had based Methodism's expansion upon the kind of strategic insights we thought *we* had discovered. *The Celtic Way of Evangelism* (Abingdon Press, 2000) featured the strategic insights behind Christianity's greatest sustained mission to pre-Christian European peoples. *Leading and Managing a Growing Church* (Abingdon Press, 2000) informed a congregation's growth from ancillary literatures.

I have also written books more from an apostolic perspective, such as *How to Reach Secular People* (Abingdon Press, 1992), *Church for the Unchurched* (Abingdon Press, 1996), and *Radical Outreach: The Recovery of Apostolic Ministry and Evangelism* (Abingdon Press, 2003), but Church Growth lore was indispensable in those reflections. Although I may have been the first Protestant writer in evangelization to feature the term *apostolic*, it has become a trendy term in recent years; but, alas, the term is now attached to *many* interests. Some writers believe that they see in the apostolic period reflected in the New Testament a precedent for the authority their clergy claim, or the doctrines they affirm, or the liturgy they celebrate, or the "gifts" they feature, or for worshiping on Saturday, or for worshiping without musical instruments, and so on—and hence they proclaim that their way is the apostolic way.

Some of those writers apparently looked into the apostolic pool and saw their own reflections; others present promising insights. In any case, I have no horse in any of those races. My main focus is on the kind of missional congregational life in which the church understands itself as an *apostolate*—"sent out" by the Lord of the Harvest to pre-Christian populations. I believe that attaching the apostolic label to *any* other concern, however valid, is majoring on the minors. I suppose I am also challenging the unquestioned assumption in many church leaders that their church and how they "do church" are exactly what Jesus and the apostles originally had in mind!

Despite the recent confusion around the term, I have continued to invite churches to become apostolic by rediscovering *the mission* of earliest Christianity and *adapting it* to their context. I have adhered to this obsession in a period when many church leaders have recognized that the church's very survival requires change of some kind; as Dietrich Bonhoeffer observed, "The rusty swords of the old world are powerless to combat the evils of today and tomorrow." In the last thirty years, many books have proposed new identities for churches and new ways of "doing church." I once made a list of more than forty such proposals; writers have conceived of boomer churches, contemporary churches, innovative churches, user-friendly churches, metachurches, seven-day-a-week churches, healthy churches, organic churches, seeker churches, purpose-driven churches, missional churches, and many other flavors.

Many of those models have featured good advice for church leaders trying to chart a new course across a changing landscape, but, to vary the metaphor, they typically spotlight only one precious stone within the mosaic. The missional church literature offered marvelous insights theologically, but most readers, once they decided to become missional, still had no idea what to *do*. (Some churches just bought the language; they said they were now missional, but nothing else had changed!) In any case, no model presenting itself as an alternative to the traditionalist church has demonstrated the power to stick beyond a half-generation. The apostolic principle, however, has demonstrated adhesive power since the earliest Christian movement. From the movement's beginning, we have known that a true church is (in ascending order) "one, holy, catholic, and apostolic."

Peter Drucker once taught us that there is one question that an organization's leaders need to ask often: What is our main business? (His second recommended question was: How is business?) C. S. Lewis in *Mere Christianity* offered an eloquent interpretation of our main business: "The Church exists for nothing else but to draw men into Christ, to make them little Christs. If they are not doing that, all the cathedrals, clergy, missions, sermons, even the Bible itself, are simply a waste of time. . . . It is even doubtful, you know, whether the whole universe was created for any other purpose."[1]

◆   ◆   ◆   ◆

Apostolic Christianity's main business is to advance *that* agenda; the field of church growth helps us discover *how* to fulfill that agenda. This book will demonstrate that the Church Growth perspective informs *how* we help fulfill that agenda in *every* mission field, including North America's fields.

I need to make two key points as explicit as I can: (1) Leaders are unlikely to lead

Christian movements without strong roots in Christian theology, especially Scripture; (2) leaders are unlikely to lead Christian movements if all they know is theology. An analogy should clarify this indispensable insight.

National Public Radio featured a professor of botany who had retired to fulfill a dream. He wanted to grow his own great Victorian garden, like he had admired in England. He applied all he had learned from botany books, journals, experiments, laboratories, and greenhouses. Five years later his garden was not a wasteland, but no one would have mistaken it for a great Victorian garden. A lifetime in botany had not prepared him for myriad issues around soils and rocks, flooding and drought, crows and other birds, moles and other subterranean critters, beetles and aphids and other insects, and a hundred other "pests" that he'd never observed in any greenhouse. His dream was further sabotaged as each plant species proved vulnerable to its own diseases. Those decades spent in botany had not fully prepared him for "the real world."

The botanist returned to England to revisit several of the great Victorian gardens. He now experienced one new revolutionary discovery: *all* of the great Victorian gardens had great Victorian gardeners! This time around, he interviewed them. They were, indeed, schooled in botany; they were also astonishingly knowledgeable in meteorology, soil biology, ornithology, entomology, chemistry, and other bodies of insight (acquired from schooling, reading, mentoring, networking, or experience), without which great Victorian gardens would have been impossible. Now he understood why his university had encouraged students to study several fields!

The botany analogy suggests that evangelism and mission and other ministries are complex challenges for which knowledge in theology is necessary but not enough. Informed by theology alone, most church leaders by themselves cannot figure out how to do *any* ministry with the greatest possible effectiveness. Church leaders also need adequate understanding of personality and culture, communication and human relations, life in organizations and communities, planning and managing, and more. As in brain surgery, portrait painting, orchestra conducting, and gardening, issues around information, approach, method, and skill *matter*—and they matter much more than some people think they should.

Church Growth knowledge, based on studies of effective apostolic churches and movements, can position and inform church leaders for significant growth. A Church Growth book cannot, of course, prescribe *exactly* how to reach the new residents on the next block who drive an Oldsmobile. Church Growth is a field much like rhetorical theory. Aristotle never claimed to teach a speaker exactly how to convince a specific legislature to support a specific tax policy; he taught us how "to discover, in [any] given situation, the available means of persuasion." Likewise, Church Growth knowledge helps Christian leaders understand the mission field entrusted to them, and helps them discover the likely, even probable ways to reach the people. So this book addresses the serious question of *how* churches make sense of their mission field and the "harvest" within it, and how churches plan and proceed to be effective in their local mission. That is the Church Growth Movement's main contribution; we do the research and reflection to answer the *how* question for church leaders who want to take their main business seriously.

◆　　　◆　　　◆　　　◆

When I have mentioned this project to colleagues and church leaders, they have indulged in one line of questioning more than any other: "Why another Church Growth book? That is *so* 1970s!" I am aware of three answers.

1. A new Church Growth text is needed because *much of the "best stuff" has been forgotten*. Many church leaders a generation ago knew more about how to reach people and grow churches than their successors know today. Today's leaders need Church Growth's strategic perspective more than ever, but they did not inherit the lore they need to inform their mission. Today I meet more church leaders who are strategically clueless than ever before. Occasionally, however, I meet church leaders who continue to read some of the older normative Church Growth books and their congregations thrive. Bil Cornelius, for instance, started the (Southern Baptist) Bay Area Fellowship in Corpus Christi, Texas, in 1997. He and his leaders read several of the "classic" Church Growth books and put together an informed local mission. A decade later they were receiving several hundred new Christians per year and their congregations served more than five thousand people per weekend.

Church Growth's strategic vision and insights have been forgotten in some of the most unlikely places. Once, for instance, Church Growth's leaders were clear that in cross-cultural mission a Christian presence in the host population is not enough. Merely loving and serving the people without also planting and growing churches, and deploying Christian nationals in ministry to their own people, perpetuates dependence upon the missionaries, the sending church, and foreign funding. Church Growth leaders, and many other leaders in world mission, labeled such an approach "paternalism"; that generation of mission leaders avoided paternalism like the plague.

This understanding was substantially lost in the leadership transition to the next generation. Today many missions accentuate a range of presence ministries that once would have received more strategic scrutiny. My own daughter and her family devoted eight years of ministry to street children in Galati, Romania. It is compassionate, demanding, exhausting, and heroic Christian ministry. Fuller Theological Seminary's School of Intercultural Studies, once the epicenter of strategic mission thought, now features and prepares hundreds of people for ministries of presence in struggling populations. The presence ministries of compassionate Christian servants are laudable; but if presence without producing an indigenous church was paternalistic thirty or forty years ago, the policy may be paternalistic today.

Most knowledge in all fields, including mission, is not simply cumulative; much is added—but some is lost—from one generation to the next.

2. A new Church Growth text is needed because *many church leaders never understood the term "Church Growth" the first time around*. Without actually studying it, they attached to it whatever meanings the term stimulated in their minds. I discovered, in that period, how widespread anti-intellectualism was (and still is) in church leadership. As Dean Kelley once made clear, "Church Growth" is *not really* about church growth! Growth in a church is a clue or an *indicator* of several possible realities (to be explained in chapter 1). This nuanced claim escaped at least half of all church leaders.

Let's indulge for a moment. Ordinarily, we are fairly accustomed to many names not meaning exactly what they first suggest. For instance, baby oil is not made out of babies and its usefulness is not restricted to babies; the cold war was not a war; American football only occasionally involves the foot in contact with the ball; political science is not a science; lipstick does not stick. Furthermore, some names have socially attached meanings that are very different than new English speakers usually expect: a boxing ring is actually square; we drive on a parkway and park on a driveway; the purpose of a wet suit is to keep you dry; a bulldog is not a bull and not much of a dog (!); and when people submit to their physician's "practice," they expect more than that. Furthermore, terms like "shaggy-dog story," "the missionary position," "friendly fire," "mission accomplished," and "Microsoft Works" may not mean *at all* what they seem to mean! We are usually aware that such language can be tricky, so we often investigate what words actually mean.

Occasionally, however, people succumb to naive realism, especially in their peer groups where they *decide together* what something "really means." For instance, this preface is being written two weeks before the 2008 presidential election. Many people, conversing in their peer groups, coalitions, and networks, have created the shared perception that Barack Obama is a "Muslim," a "socialist," and probably "anti-American" or a "terrorist." They are, at least at the moment, supremely confident that their group invention represents reality.

When we advocated the Church Growth approach in the 1970s and 1980s, we often met a similar pattern. (I discovered that people across the ideological spectrum are capable of naive realism.) In the climate of the time, some church leaders resisted Church Growth's use of membership statistics and graphs because, they said, it reminded them of "business," and, in any case, they almost seemed more interested in membership decline than in growth; decline was proof that you were "prophetic," and if the church declined enough it would become a (righteous) "remnant."

Some church leaders were hyperanxious about *anything* related to mission or evangelism. In such a climate, church leader groups sometimes decided that Church Growth was imposing business methods or mechanical engineering upon churches, that its goal was success (or even triumphalism), and that it was probably racist. Since people tended to be *really* confident of their shared conclusions, we were never able to get across to many church leaders (who seemed to need this knowledge the most) what Church Growth was really about. They ran and reacted with the meanings the term triggered within their shared imagination. So the first chapter of this book proposes to introduce and *re*introduce the Church Growth perspective for informing a congregation's mission.

3. A new Church Growth text is needed because *we have learned some important things about effective mission and evangelism since Donald McGavran made his enduring contribution.* This book's chief purpose is to *advance* McGavran's perspective in a changing world and for a new generation. This project does not pretend to take the place of McGavran's *Understanding Church Growth.* So, in contrast to his classic, the focus of this book is different in three ways:

- This book focuses more on the West's mission fields and less on the two-thirds world.

- Of McGavran's four "types" of Church Growth (internal, expansion, extension, and bridging), this book focuses very largely on expansion growth.

- This book does not review as much literature from other writers as does McGavran's text. I could have done that (I have listed in chapter 1 the names of some of the writers worth drawing from), but it would have taken another year and this book is already too long. (Alas, some chapters are also too long, but mercifully the long chapters are divided into subtitled "chapterettes.") So I am mainly presenting the conclusions from my own research and reflection, hoping that this will not be the only Church Growth book someone reads.

◆　　　◆　　　◆　　　◆

Moreover, I have written this book at a time when most of us in the Church Growth Movement have mellowed; we now present our insights in more nuanced ways than before. For instance, we are now clearer than before that the key term *growth* is *not* as simple—and its meaning is not as self-evident—as we first thought. Some of us now sympathize with our critics' charge that not all growth is good, and some is even undesirable. Some growth may be analogous to "fat"—as when a church receives new members who are not serious disciples, or when a low-expectation church is content with its people dutifully attending church while the pastor circulates as everyone's chaplain. A church, like any body, has a limit to the amount of "fat" that it can drag along and be healthy. Furthermore, some growth may be analogous to "malignancy"—as when a liberal church welcomes new members who have not turned from non-Christian gods and worldviews, or when a conservative church welcomes people who confuse beliefs with faith, or nationalism with Christianity, or who live more by a legalistic ethic than a love and justice ethic. A church is severely limited in the amount of "malignancy" it can carry without jeopardizing the whole body.

Finally, we recall McGavran's wisdom that there will be periods and contexts in which war, oppression, disease, or starvation are rampant, in which Christianity's social mandate may take some priority over the evangelistic mandate. We now know that there are more such periods and contexts than we once perceived, that the Great Commandment—as well as the Great Commission—is a mandate, and that we are now more earnest than before that God's "will be done, on earth as it is in heaven." Furthermore, the social mandate is now more of a conscious priority in the world church, including the more evangelical traditions, than it has been in a long time. Essentially, however, this is not a new obsession; we are recovering the evangelical tradition that once populated the movements that worked to abolish the slave trade and then slavery itself.

Although informing evangelization within and across cultures is still Church Growth's indispensable contribution, there are two ways in which the Church Growth tradition is destined to advance both the evangelistic mandate and the social mandate. (1) We know that the goal of evangelism is more than just getting people into churches and enrolled for heaven. Churches are called to produce the kind of disciples who know that they are the "salt of the earth" and "the light of the world." In the fallen societies of the world, negligible Christian minorities have no influence; but when churches grow enough kingdom people to constitute a critical mass, they can exercise considerable influence. An evangelism that communicates the gospel and its ethic can provide the army of committed people who will help a social cause prevail. (2) Someday, scholars and leaders whose first interest is advancing life, justice, and peace will learn from us how to expand the ranks of the committed to achieve that critical mass, *and* as they conduct something like the Church Growth tradition's field research, they will study enough churches that are helping transform communities and societies to clarify the methods and approaches that can impact communities and societies everywhere.

◆   ◆   ◆   ◆

Some material in the book has been presented in a range of institutions, including lectureships at the Overseas Ministries Study Center in New Haven, Connecticut; South America Theological Seminary's Jethro Institute in Londrina, Brazil; Methodist Theological Seminary and Hyupsung University in Seoul, Korea; Gardner-Webb University in North Carolina; and in Church Growth courses in Asbury Theological Seminary's E. Stanley Jones School of World Mission and Evangelism; and in many field seminars. Through the miracle of feedback, many people who heard or read earlier versions have contributed to any clarity or usefulness in this published form, for which I am grateful.

I also express gratitude for Bob Ratcliff, editor of professional and academic books at Abingdon Press, for the historian's eye and the shared commitment that he brings to the publication of my books.

(Re)Introducing Church Growth to a New Generation

Once upon a time, in Europe's medieval Christendom period, virtually every person in every village was a baptized and catechized Christian. As that era recedes into the haze of memory, as Europe and North America (and most societies on other continents) become more and more secular, as our communities are increasingly populated by people who have no idea what Christians believe and live for, church leaders are discovering that their communities, in which confessing Christian faith and involvement in a church was once the social custom, have become secular mission fields. The United States, for instance, has *at least* 180 million functionally secular people who have never been substantially influenced by any serious version of the Christian faith. That makes the United States the largest mission field in the Western Hemisphere and the third largest on Earth.

The secularity of Western communities and societies is not a brand-new phenomenon. The secularization of the West began several centuries ago. Sustained cultural events—like the Renaissance and the Enlightenment, the rise of science and cities, and the invasions of many religions and ideologies—slowly, but surely, removed the "home-field advantage" that the Western church had enjoyed for centuries. Secularization, however, began stampeding across much of Europe following the First World War; the process increased in North America following the Second World War and then gained momentum following the Korean War.[1]

The chief product of secularization is secular people. More and more people, in all of our communities, have lived their whole lives beyond the influence of churches. They have never been substantially influenced by the Christian faith in any viable form; they have no Christian memory, no church in their background to return to one day. They are not, however, blank slates; they are not usually people of no religion at all. The lens through which they perceive ultimate reality and the purpose of life has been influenced by a range of religions, philosophies, ideologies, and spiritualities—from astrology to Zen, from capitalism to Marxism, from new age to Scientology, from ESP to UFOs, and so on. No one can now keep up with all of the religious options that have crowded into Western societies since Christianity lost its cartel, since the church's position in society changed from one of monopoly to one of competition.

◆   ◆   ◆   ◆

This secularized context presents a formidable challenge for Western church leaders. In the 1970s, when Donald McGavran's Church Growth thought became known in the United States, the book by McGavran and Win Arn, *How to Grow a Church*,[2] demonstrated that the strategic principles for effective evangelism that McGavran

1

(and others) had discovered in Asia, Africa, Latin America, and Oceania could be adapted to North American and European fields as well.

McGavran had served as the founding dean of Fuller Theological Seminary's School of World Mission, following his first career as a Christian Church (Disciples of Christ) missionary and mission executive in central India. One day, in the early 1930s, McGavran was studying the annual reports of churches in his region and he discovered that only about 5 percent of the region's churches were growing by receiving new Christians into their ranks; the other 95 percent were stagnant or declining in membership strength.

McGavran reflected upon the growing 5 percent and wondered *why* they were growing in a field where 95 percent were not. Over time, he refined and nuanced the question (a process that some of us have continued): *Why* do some churches grow? What are the *causes* of church growth? What are the *barriers* or the *sicknesses* that prevent growth? What are the *reproducible principles* that account for a congregation's growth? What do the leaders of growing churches *know* that leaders of nongrowing churches do not know, or at least do not take seriously? What do the growing churches *do* that nongrowing churches do not do? Or, if they both do it, how do the growing churches do it *differently*? (Those questions about *knowledge*, *approach*, and *style* have driven our research for several decades.)

At least three prominent mission thinkers preceded McGavran's quest. Roland Allen, an early-twentieth-century Anglican, reflected from his experience (cut short by illness) in northern China. In *Missionary Methods: St. Paul's or Ours?* and in *The Spontaneous Expansion of the Church*, he contended that a mission's policies and approaches really matter, and he anticipated some of McGavran's strategic themes. Kenneth Scott Latourette, McGavran's professor at Yale Divinity School, spent much of the second quarter of the twentieth century producing the seven-volume *History of the Expansion of Christianity* (and other books) that informed such questions historically. Then, a book based upon field research by a contemporary in India, Methodist missionary J. Waskom Pickett's *Christian Mass Movements in India*, helped focus the rest of McGavran's life.[3] McGavran said, "I lit my candle at Pickett's fire!" He stood on Pickett's shoulders while also drawing from the behavioral science research methods he had acquired in PhD studies at Columbia University.

Pickett had surveyed thousands of India's converts and interviewed hundreds. McGavran did not rely on surveys as much as Pickett did; he employed more historical analysis, field observation, and extensive interviews with converts. McGavran collected data and reflected for twenty years before he published much. Then the 1955 publication of *The Bridges of God*[4] exploded into the world of mission thinkers and leaders who were abandoning the earlier "colonial" approach to mission and were open to alternative approaches. The three editions of *Understanding Church Growth* (1970, 1980, and 1990) distill McGavran's enduring perspective.

In addition to Pickett, other McGavran contemporaries contributed to the Church Growth school. Eugene Nida and Alan Tippett advanced the knowledge from anthropological research. Ralph Winter contributed major historical and strategic perspectives. C. Peter Wagner explored Pentecostal growth for its insights and became the leading public interpreter of the field. Several writers advanced our understanding of church growth in specific cultural regions, such as Roy Shearer (Kore' Yamamori (Japan), J. T. Seamands (India), William Read (Latin America,. Hedlund (Italy), and Jim Montgomery (Philippines).

Somewhat later, a range of people reflected upon Church Growth in the West. Their contributions are too important to hide their names in a footnote. This range of people includes Win and Charles Arn, Wendell Belew, Charles Chaney, Francis DuBose, Bill Easum, Carl George, Eddie Gibbs, Kirk Hadaway, Kent Hunter, Dean Kelley, Robert Logan, Gary McIntosh, Thom Ranier, Dan Reeves, David Roozen, Ebbie Smith, Ed Stetzer, Elmer Towns, John Vaughan, Waldo Werning, Bob Whitesel, Flavil Yeakley, and the present writer. From the perspectives of other disciplines, other scholars have addressed some of the same questions, including Michael Green (early church history); Stephen Neill (mission history); Roger Greenway, Harvie Conn, and Ray Bakke (urban mission); David Barrett (world Christianity); Dean Kelley and Rodney Stark (sociology); and Lyle Schaller (congregational studies).[5]

How does chuch gro— is sure a control

What Do We Mean by "Church Growth"?

As suggested in the preface, we need to introduce Church Growth principles to younger church leaders—and also to some senior leaders who did not "get it" the first time around. People have often misunderstood and resisted what Church Growth thought can do for their mission. One cause of the confusion (and resistance) is semantic; when people first hear of a field like "Hermeneutics" or "Symbolic Interactionism," the terms trigger *no* meaning in their minds, so they have to look them up. When, however, they hear of a field like "Organization Development" or "Church Growth," the terms *do* connote some meaning in their minds and, if two or more agree on what it must mean, they assume they are right and they react from the meaning they attach to the term. Most often, when people hear "Church Growth," they think of numbers, and their grapevine says, "Church Growth is just about numbers." (In the American Society for Church Growth, after a quarter century we know we have lost the semantic battle; so we may change the organization's name to something like the Great Commission Research Network.)

Unconscious semantic confusion is not, however, the only cause of confusion and resistance. Some church leaders, for instance, dislike the fact that Church Growth people may employ statistics and even graphs to help make sense of a church's (or a movement's) growth; statistics and graphs remind them of business—and business methods, they say, are incompatible with Christianity. Since they usually believe that church leaders only need to know theology, they also resist insights from other fields.[6] In the real world, however, *effective* leadership's knowledge base is increasingly interdisciplinary. Theology is not *all* one needs to know to be effective in ministry or mission, any more than anatomy is *all* one needs to know to do brain surgery, or political philosophy to manage a city, or botany to grow a flower garden.

People from the other side can also take their shots. Some church leaders dislike the fact that Church Growth people mainly do qualitative field research, such as historical analysis, observation, and interviews. (McGavran interviewed thousands of converts and said he learned more from them about what actually happens in effective evangelism than from most of the books that prescribe how evangelism "ought" to be done!) These detractors say that Church Growth needs to be more scientific; and they decree that *only* quantitative data (expressed in statistics and graphs) is worthy of a science.

Again from both sides, two more reasons for resistance to Church Growth are more or less theological, and both sides react to McGavran's teaching that Christianity's main business is the kind of *evangelization* that reaches, and makes disciples among, pre-Christian populations. One side insists (or assumes) that a church's main business is *not* evangelizing pagans; it is shepherding church members and their children, and protecting churches from pagans, a fallen world, and heresy. The membership goal of such churches is to maintain their current membership, but they typically decline. (They lose 5 to 8 percent of their people per year as some people transfer to other churches, or die, or revert to the world. If a church is not reaching out enough to replace the members it loses, it declines.)

The other side insists that the church does have a responsibility for the world, but its main business is to advance every Christian cause (like peace and justice) *except* evangelism: Great Commandment—yes; Great Commission—no. Donald McGavran was sympathetic with the social reformers. He observed, however, that to move a society toward justice, a Christian social movement needs a critical mass of people who own the kingdom vision. You cannot change a society with fewer and fewer people to work for change; and you increase the ranks of Christ-followers mainly by evangelizing in some appropriate way.[7] In the 1960s and 1970s, these issues were so heated that McGavran wrote *The Eye of the Storm: The Great Debate in Mission*.[8] Those controversies are not raging as much today, in part because the membership strength and especially the mission personnel in the mainline traditions have declined so much that their point of view is less consequential.

◆　　◆　　◆　　◆

So what is Church Growth about, and what are the reasons for its methods?

The preface suggested that Church Growth is not really about church growth. As Dean Kelley stressed in the 1970s, a church's growth is a clue or an *indicator* of a church's probable vitality, seriousness, and effectiveness in its mission. "Church Growth" became a shorthand term for five overlapping interests that Church Growth people share. In the 1970s and 1980s, the "Church Growth" minirevolution led by Donald McGavran featured five significant perspectives to the world's churches.

1. McGavran helped many churches recover their "main business," which is not merely serving the members of the gathered churches; churches are entrusted with the apostolic assignment of reaching pre-Christian people—and peoples. McGavran declared, "It is God's will that his church grow, that his lost children be found." (So the growth of a church, particularly its conversion growth rate, is an *indicator* of whether or not it is prioritizing its main business.)

2. McGavran perceived that the chief objective of both evangelism (within a culture) and mission (across cultures) is not merely to establish a loving presence among

the people, or to proclaim the gospel, or to elicit decisions; rather, it is to communicate the meaning of the gospel and to *make disciples*, especially new disciples. This objective is essentially achieved when people experience two significant life changes: (1) They start following Jesus Christ as Lord, AND (2) they are incorporated into some community of the body of Christ. These two changes may occur in either order! (The church's numerical growth is a good *indicator* that the second objective is being achieved; it is a less than sufficiently reliable indicator of whether the first objective is being achieved.)

3. McGavran and his Church Growth colleagues advanced the *strategy* perspective in world mission. Many mission agencies would no longer blindly perpetuate their traditional activities (such as literacy, education, medicine, and agriculture) in the assumption that, of course, their activities were advancing the Great Commission. Reflective agencies became clearer about their objectives; more self-critical about whether their activities were achieving those objectives; and more strategic, flexible, and innovative in pursuit of their objectives. (When we attach specific and measurable goals to our objectives, the later numbers *indicate* whether we are achieving our objectives.)

4. McGavran raised the question about *effective evangelism*. He observed that, in evangelism, "we know what *ought* to reach people." He dared to ask questions like, "What approaches, methods, and ministries, in what kinds of contexts, *actually* reach people, gather harvests, and make new disciples?" (Again, if we are measuring the right things, such as people joining churches by confession of new faith, the numbers will *indicate* our relative effectiveness.)

5. Church Growth people have employed extensive *field research* to inform effective mission and evangelism. As Church Growth field researchers studied hundreds of growing churches, in many lands, tongues, and cultures, and as they interviewed thousands of new converts, they discovered many principles behind the Christian faith's expansion (and decline). In time, their insights have informed Christianity's outreach in unprecedented ways. (The numerical *indicators* of significant growth or decline point us to the places for field research!)

From Four Types of Church Growth to Six

The acknowledgment in the preface that some growth may be analogous to fat or even to malignancy, and therefore may not be desirable, has helped us become clearer about the types of Church Growth that *are* desirable. Donald McGavran observed that Christian movements grow in multiple ways. Collaboration between McGavran, Ralph Winter, and Peter Wagner developed one of the Church Growth field's most essential and enduring paradigms: churches grow essentially in four ways.

1. Internal Growth

2. Expansion Growth

3. Extension Growth

4. Bridging Growth

Whereas this typology has endured for forty years and has proved perennially useful, it is no longer sufficient to explain many of the growing churches and especially the Christian movements that we now observe. For instance, when a church starts a second campus, does that represent extension growth? Or when a church is growing with contagion, is that merely expansion growth, or is another dynamic discernible? Our understanding of the ways in which churches grow has evolved; with experience and reflection, we can now nuance our understandings within the paradigm in more precise and useful ways by adding two additional categories for understanding the ways churches grow:

5. Catalytic Growth

6. Proliferation Growth

Internal Growth

In *Understanding Church Growth*, McGavran defined *internal growth* as "increase in sub-groups within existing churches, i.e., increase of competent Christians, men and women who know the Bible and practice the Christian faith. They move from marginal to ardent belief."[9] Subsequent writers have expanded and nuanced our understanding of internal growth and have generated alternative terms for this type of growth more than any of the other types. McGavran's colleague at Fuller, Alan Tippett, preferred terms like "quality growth" and especially "organic growth," and he imported anthropologist Anthony Wallace's emphasis on the importance, for long-term strength, of revitalization movements within churches. Peter Wagner's glossary in *Church Growth: State of the Art* defined internal church growth as individual "Christians growing in their faith and in living out their Christian commitment"; whereas he defined the related term "qualitative growth" more corporately as "the collective improvement in Christian commitment and ministry among the members of a given local church."[10]

Some of us have used the term to refer to all the ways in which existing churches become more rooted, faithful, compassionate, or powerful churches. In *To Spread the Power: Church Growth in the Wesleyan Spirit*, I suggested:

> Internal Growth refers to the growth in depth, quality, or vitality of an already existing congregation. When the nominal members discover the living Christ and begin following him, when the members are more rooted in scripture or more disciplined in prayer, when the people become more loving or empowered, or more attuned to God's will for peace and justice and finding the lost, then the church is experiencing internal growth.[11]

In the 1970s and 1980s, Church Growth people did not do as much research and writing on internal growth as they did on expansion, extension, and bridging growth, largely because the writers in spiritual formation and church renewal were addressing this challenge as, more recently, the church health writers have done.

Of the church health writers, Christian Schwarz has been remarkably specific in profiling the characteristics of healthy churches:[12]

1. Empowering Leadership

2. Gift-oriented Ministry

3. Passionate Spirituality

4. Functional Structures

5. Inspiring Worship

6. Holistic Small Groups

7. Need-oriented Evangelism

8. Loving Relationships[13]

◆   ◆   ◆   ◆

Some Church Growth writers take serious issue with the "renewal" people and the "health" people, who seem to advise a church or denomination to become renewed or healthy enough *first*, before getting involved in outreach and mission. Their prescription ignores one brute fact: the church or denomination *never* feels healthy enough to move to the second stage! Nevertheless, the church renewal and spiritual formation fields have stimulated or contributed at least three new insights for informing internal church growth.

1. We are now clear that one reason existing churches often lack sufficient health and need renewing is because they have not been reaching out or involved in wider mission. Lack of outreach, theologically, is rooted in disobedience to Christ's Great Commission, or at least in a reluctance to cooperate with the church's main business. A gazillion prayer meetings and daily devotionals will not free spirits that are stuck in fundamental disobedience. On the contrary, involvement, conversation, and ministry with lost people—who look to us for the signs of credibility—drive us into Christian maturity in ways that spending all of one's time with the saints cannot. To be specific, we learn more about what the gospel means by framing and explaining it for pre-Christian people than we would likely learn from an entire degree program in desk theology. Furthermore, Church Growth people have discovered that nothing renews a lethargic congregation like getting involved in wider mission and receiving a stream of converts entering their ranks.

2. My research that resulted in *The Celtic Way of Evangelism* produced some distinctive insights for internal growth. For instance, for the ancient Celtic Christian movement, spiritual formation was a means to prepare and empower us for ministry and mission, much more than just for our own spiritual experiences and fulfillment. The Celtic movement took seriously Paul's mandate to the Thessalonian Christians to "pray without ceasing." So, it was even more important to pray *while* you were studying the Scriptures, preparing a lesson, traveling on a mission, or serving someone than to keep a daily ritual. Moreover, the Celtic saints taught us to harness our imaginations for prayer, as in Patrick's famous Breastplate Prayer, in which he imagines or visualizes "Christ with me, Christ before me, Christ behind me; Christ within me, Christ beneath me, Christ above me,"[14] and so on.

3. Reg Johnson's research has provided the significant breakthrough insight that, contrary to the usual expectation in churches, one single approach does *not* fit all people in our quest for spiritual maturity; we do not all grow in Christ in the same way. Johnson's research demonstrates that one's most natural approach to supernatural formation partly depends on one's personality type, based on the thought of Carl Jung and the well-known Myers-Briggs Personality Type Inventory. (So, for instance, although we are only somewhat different from one another, and saints are typically formed through a range of spiritual practices, introverts more naturally meet God in solitude, while extroverts more naturally meet God when "two or more" are together. For other types, the experience of the Spirit is especially mediated through music, sacred space, movement, visual art, biography, theology, liturgy, or pageantry. From Johnson's application of the Myers-Briggs typology, the opportunity is now given to identify which of eight basic approaches to spiritual formation best fits one's personality.[15]

Three additional insights about internal growth and spiritual formation may be approaching consensus. First, there is more emphasis that the people of God need to accept more responsibility for their own formation and maturity in Christ. There is a limit to how much a church's many ministries can do *for* people. The second derives from the field of symbolic interactionism, which has featured our "self-talk," and how our ongoing internal conversations lead to most of the feelings we experience and most of the decisions we make. This field of inquiry has led to renewed interest in *memorizing* the biblical texts, wisdom sayings, poetry, and other material that ought to be salient in our consciousness and internal conversation. Third, the most indispensable outcome of formation is people who now seek and do the will of God. If a devotional life only reinforces people's therapeutic and moralistic narcissism, Christianity will never be producing its fair share of "apostles, prophets, saints, and martyrs."

Expansion Growth

A local church experiences *expansion church growth* when new people enter the church's ranks and become new members. McGavran gave this category three strategic subdivisions: (a) *Biological growth* occurs when the children of church members come up through the ranks and are received or confirmed into the church. (b) *Transfer growth* occurs when the church receives active Christians into its membership from another church, whether a church of its own denomination or another. (c) *Conversion growth* occurs when the church receives new Christians "from the world."

Since McGavran's period, the usefulness of adding a fourth strategic subdivision has become obvious: (d) *restoration growth.* For decades, the annual statistical report that many churches sent to denominational headquarters included the number of people received into the church's membership "on confession of faith or restored." McGavran observed that such umbrella categories conceal as much as they reveal. If, say, a church reported fifty new members in that category, whom was the church really reaching? The category combined three populations: children who joined from the confirmation class; AND teens and adults who joined "from the world" and therefore represented conversion growth; AND people who had once confessed faith and been involved in churches but who then lapsed for such a long time that their former church's membership role no longer included them and, therefore, could not transfer them.

In very recent years, the form for United Methodist churches asks them to report the number received "on profession of faith" and, in the next column, the number received "by reaffirmation of faith." This denomination's churches now specifically count their restored believers who'd been lapsed for long enough to have no church to transfer from. This distinction between conversion growth and restoration growth is strategically important.

Conversion growth should represent effective outreach to people who have little or no Christian memory, no prior personal history of discipleship; with such people the church cannot assume much prior knowledge or much residue of Christian insight and must introduce "Christianity 101."

Restoration growth should represent effective outreach to people who have a background of faith to return to one day. With such people, the church can often presuppose some background knowledge and experience; but for some their remembered experiences may be negative, that is, they may remember church as boring, irrelevant, legalistic, or even punitive. For some the memories are even painful. Such people do not usually return to a church that is much like the one they once dropped out of; when they return, they typically turn to a different type of church and a different type of church experience. (Both populations, converts and restored believers, will often have to experience "belonging before believing.")

In the United States, including all four subdivisions of expansion growth, only about 20 out of every 100 of the nation's 360,000 churches are growing, and 17 of the 20 are growing primarily by biological growth (sometimes called "Vatican Roulette"!) or transfer growth, or both. More than two out of the 20 grow by biological, transfer, and restoration growth. Less than one out of 20 growing churches (which is to say less than 1 percent of all the churches in the United States) grow significantly from conversion growth in a given year. As McGavran used to say, "Conversion growth is where we need to put in our emphasis." Conversion growth is, after all, an outcome of apostolic Christianity's main assignment. Chapters 5 and 6 of this book are devoted to what we know about the outreach approaches that help produce conversion growth. Chapter 2 profiles the kind of church that produces an apostolic people and best receives seekers and converts.

If, indeed, the Lord of the Harvest calls many churches to experience more expansion growth, and especially more conversion growth, some criteria for what conversion growth entails are necessary.[16]

- *Substantial Growth.* Some churches expand more substantially than others. I am defining substantial growth as a church *doubling* its membership strength in *ten years*. Such a church might average receiving, in each year of the decade, 13 percent of the church's prior membership as new members while losing perhaps 6 percent of its prior members to death, transfer, and reversion to the world; so a church that finished last year with 100 members that receives 13 new members this year, while losing six, experiences 7 percent net growth. A church averaging 7 percent net growth per year essentially doubles in a decade.

- *Movemental Growth.* A church that *doubles* its membership strength in *five years* is experiencing movemental growth. Such a church would receive, in a typical year, at least 20 new members (per 100 previous members) while still losing about 6 percent of its members. A net growth of 14 percent per year essentially doubles the church's membership strength in five years.

- *Apostolic Growth.* A church which is experiencing either substantial or movemental growth is also experiencing apostolic growth if *at least* 15 percent of the new members represent bona fide conversion growth from the world. (One would be tempted to peg that standard higher, but churches that bring in many converts also retain more of their children. They also attract more restored Christians and more transfers.)

Although causal connections are difficult to demonstrate, there are reasons to believe that the Church Growth movement's trumpet call to prioritize conversion growth has provided focus for *at least* half of the churches in the land who now experience much more conversion growth than before, and has prodded many other churches and church leaders toward a more apostolic orientation.

Extension Growth

Extension growth occurs when a church (or a judicatory or a denomination) plants a new church to reach people that the mother church would like to reach but cannot reach, in substantial numbers at least, because they are "too far away." The target population may live beyond reasonable traveling distance of the mother church, or they may represent a subculture, a socioeconomic class of people, a language or a dialect, or a condition (such as illiteracy or addiction) that would raise invisible barriers that the mother church could not overcome. So, traditionally, the mother church or judicatory buys some land, underwrites a founding pastor, deploys some core members from the mother church, builds a first building, and so on.

When the American Church Growth Movement surfaced in the 1970s, many denominations had been propagandized into assuming that church planting was no longer trendy; so, despite the country's mobile populations, increasing urbanization, and ethnic immigrations, denominations were planting fewer new churches than ever before. Win Arn used to dramatize the effects of such policies by calculating the approximate number of churches in the United States per 10,000 people.

1900: 27 churches per 10,000 people

1950: 17 churches per 10,000 people

2000: 12 churches per 10,000 people

Such data, however, may obscure almost as much as they reveal because new churches over time have not all been created equal. The 1900 figure reflects the 1880–

1905 period, when denominations averaged 4,000 new churches per year. Many of the churches were established to serve such populations as immigrants from Europe, freed slaves, people moving to the cities, and people moving west. Churches were typically planted on one acre (two if they attached a cemetery). A new church in a city usually served a neighborhood.

The 1950 figure reflects the 1945–60 period when the denominations started about 3,000 churches per year, often on three or four acres, to serve veterans of World War II and people moving to the cities and, increasingly, to the suburbs. Many people now had cars; so, while some attendees parked on the street, churches now also provided parking. Many new churches in cities served newer neighborhoods, but some "regional" churches were now established on major traffic arteries to serve a whole region of the city.

New churches in more recent years are different in many ways. Many are started by a church planting team, rather than by a lone-ranger pastor. Fewer new neighborhood churches are planted (except churches for ethnic minority neighborhoods); more regional churches are planted. New churches, now, are typically started on sites of at least ten acres, and often much more; they often plan from the beginning to feature multiple congregations, and they provide at least 50 parking places for every 100 people they expect to have in the facility at one time. Larger churches often provide surplus parking. Many newer churches now serve immigrants from Asia or Latin America. New churches are different in other ways. In 1960, for instance, church attendees needed 17 inches of pew to sit on; today, because of "the girthing of America" and changing comfort levels, people need 23 inches. Some churches have replaced pews with theater seats.

The biggest difference is the rise of megachurches (defined as those with 2,000 average weekly worship attendance). For most of Christianity's history, they were not possible; even if the speaker was elevated, the unaided human voice could only project to 400 to 800 people, depending on architecture and acoustics; the electronic public address system made much larger churches possible. Historically, there was also a limit to the number of people who lived close enough to walk to the church; what the public address system made possible, the automobile made feasible. So a new church today typically engages larger congregations—and multiple congregations—compared to two generations ago; and some churches now serve more populations through multiple campuses.

The referent for new churches is different enough today to nuance Win Arn's data. His data, however, obscures another fact. In 1900, about three-fourths of the population lived in town, village, and open country settings, while one-fourth lived in the cities. By 2000, the demographics had reversed—about three-fourths of the people lived in urban areas, while one-fourth lived in town and country. So, although we have about 12 churches for every 10,000 people, a disproportionate number of the nation's churches are placed where the people used to live, and not nearly enough churches serve city people. Consequently, many villages today may have a church for every 100 to 300 people, while many cities have a church for every 1,000 to 3,000 people. The number of larger churches with multiple congregations in the cities today only partly compensates for the strategic disparity; we still have too few churches reaching and serving urban populations—in the cities *and* the suburbs.

In the 1960s, many denominations virtually ceased starting new congregations. For years Church Growth people were almost alone in advocating and teaching church planting. As a range of denominations regained this emphasis to some degree, many denominations doubled or tripled their rate of new church plants. These denominations are still planting fewer churches than they once did; indeed, they are seizing less than half of the opportunities to plant new congregations that present themselves.

Meanwhile, the traditional interpretation of the extension growth category has become somewhat less useful over time because increasing numbers of churches are functioning outside of the term's traditional boundaries. On the one hand, most cities have become so multicultural and multilingual that much church planting, even in the mother church's own city, is essentially bridging growth, our next category of growth. On the other hand, we now observe many innovative expressions of the extension impulse, such as the multiplication of congregations within existing churches. Many churches, in many nations, feature a dozen or more congregations in the same church, usually in several liturgical styles, often in several languages. The new category of proliferation growth helps us account for and encourage this emergent form of church growth.

Bridging Growth

Bridging growth occurs when a church sends cross-cultural missionaries across great language and cultural barriers to start or enhance a Christian movement among a population that is very different from the people of the sending church. Historically, cross-cultural missionaries also traveled great distances to foreign nations, and that pattern continues. As cities and nations become more multicultural and multilingual, however, planting a Christian movement among, for example, Latino, Chinese, Russian, Samoan, Tamil, or Hausa people in one's own city or nation involves many dynamics of cross-cultural mission *within* the sending church's city, state, or nation.

Since the 1970s, the Church Growth Movement has championed the continuing cross-cultural mission of the nation's churches. Considering the fact that about 10,000 of the earth's approximately 30,000 "people groups"—a statistic representing more than two billion individuals speaking several thousand languages or mutually unintelligible dialects—still have no indigenous evangelizing church within their ranks, the church executives who once called for a moratorium on sending missionaries were, apparently, not familiar with the demographic facts that would inform such a policy!

Nevertheless, mission's critics sensitized many churches to refrain from sending old-school colonial-type missionaries who could not adequately distinguish between Christianity and Western "civilization," and who tended to impose Western ways and call it Christianity. The call today is for more incarnational missionaries who identify with the host cultures and work with the people to develop indigenous Christianity.

The Church Growth movement's achievement in championing the sending of contextually appropriate missionaries is mixed. Overall, with some fluctuations and exceptions, the independent mission agencies are sending more missionaries, while the official mainline denominational agencies are sending fewer. Rodney Stark, a leading sociologist of religion, explains:

The liberal American denominations...have become essentially irrelevant
American foreign mission effort. In 1880, the liberals—Congregatio
Presbyterians, Methodists, and Episcopalians—provided more than 9 missionaries out
of every 10 sent abroad from the United States.... By 1935, the liberals supplied fewer
than half of the American missionaries.... In 1996, they sent out fewer than 1 out of
20 of those registered with official mission boards.[17]

Introducing Catalytic Growth

It is time for Church Growth's most perennially useful paradigm to experience
some expansion growth for the simple reason that the established four types of Church
Growth, even with the embellishments of the years, do not sufficiently account for
much of Christianity's expansion that we now observe; but two more categories can,
with the traditional four, help us account for most of that growth. After an exhaustive
search for the right terms, two metaphors now help us identify two ways that the
church grows that the four traditional terms obscured: catalytic growth and proliferation growth. We now suggest that the church grows essentially in *six* ways:

1. Internal Growth

2. Expansion Growth

3. *Catalytic Growth >

4. *Proliferation Growth >

5. Extension Growth

6. Bridging Growth

Catalytic growth refers to a distinctive, powerful, infectious dynamic that we can
usually observe when a church is experiencing movemental growth or apostolic
growth, as defined above. We usually observe, and experience, a "catalytic" dynamic
when Christianity becomes a wider contagious movement. I am employing the term
as a metaphor, borrowed from chemistry, in which a catalyst increases the rate in a
chemical reaction. So in a crisis, for instance, a surge of adrenalin catalyzes the body
for "fight or flight." Or when an athlete ingests creatine before resistance exercise, the
creatine catalyzes the body's production of adenosine triphosphate (ATP), which
powers two or three more bench presses, which catalyzes more muscle growth. I am
told that the cocktail of multiple supplements and drugs that HIV patients now
receive is designed to catalyze the body's immune system in multiple ways.

From the earliest apostolic movement, something like catalysis is prominent and
potent in contagious Christian movements. The dynamic, like internal growth, is
essentially qualitative, but it typically results in greatly increased expansion, extension, proliferation, and bridging growth.

The catalytic principle is often involved as the faith spreads within a family, a clan,
or a peer group. Consider a case. A forty-year-old man from Chicago, from a secular

and unchurched extended family, and long addicted to alcohol, was "detoxed" and began recovery at a rehabilitation clinic. He continued in twelve-step recovery at a halfway house for six months, and then moved back home. A friend who had once boozed with him but who was now in recovery invited him to a church that featured a large sign: "Recovery Spoken Here." The church welcomed him, and he felt wanted and at home. In one of the church's twelve-step meetings, he discovered that the Higher Power he had opened to in rehab was the Holy Spirit, who now pointed him to Christ who reconciled him to the Father. Although he still carried some of the marks of "the far country," he was so profoundly changed that his family, his work peers, and several drinking buddies were astonished; they attended his baptismal service and were deeply moved. The church reached out to his family and friends, and to peers in the addictive community. Within six months, thirty were baptized as new Christians, and some of their peers, friends, and family were responding. When the people observed *miracles* that they could not deny or account for—except for God— that experience catalyzed receptivity in the souls of many people.

My book *Radical Outreach: The Recovery of Apostolic Ministry and Evangelism* has reintroduced this principle after decades—or centuries—of amnesia. *Radical Outreach* demonstrates the indispensable presence of the catalytic factor in several of history's great Christian movements and that the apostles knew this powerful principle, as did figures such as Saint Patrick and John Wesley, who recovered a strategic understanding of the dynamic. My thesis suggests that in virtually every society there is a regular or establishment population and there are also fringe populations (down-and-outers AND up-and-outers) whom the establishment people regard as "impossible" or "hopeless." Catalytic movements emerge when some of the latter populations are reached and changed; such movements may spread like wildfire.

Consider a biblical precedent. In first-century Galilee, the marginalized and allegedly hopeless populations included lepers, people who were blind, people who were deaf, prostitutes, Samaritans, the possessed, and the paralytics, as well as tax collectors ("traitors") and zealots ("terrorists"). NOTICE: Such people were on the official list of people banned from the Temple. Much of Jesus' visible public ministry was to such populations, which would have seized the attention of Galilean people. Jesus' own band of twelve included former enemies—a tax collector and a zealot; this spoke volumes. As the living miracles multiplied, so many more people became receptive that establishment Judaism and the Roman occupiers perceived Jesus' movement as a threat.

The larger principle was not lost on the disciples who became apostles. Many of the apostles reached populations widely regarded as impossible, even so-called barbarians, and even cannibal populations. The second-century apostolic traditions, for instance, tell us that Andrew reached the Scythians, who were widely regarded as more animal than human. Matthew, at the cost of his life, planted the gospel seed in the land of the Anthropophagi—cannibals; but, following Matthew's execution, the king converted and led many of his people into the faith.

This catalytic principle is expressed differently in different contexts depending on what kind of people the establishment assumes to be impossible. In eighteenth-century England, for instance, when the fencing of the land pushed many rural people out of the countryside and the new jobs of the Industrial Revolution pulled them into the cities, the established Church of England launched virtually no mission to the "common people" who now crowded the cities. Such people were not considered fit candidates for Christianization. After all, they did not dress like good church people; they had never acquired a church etiquette. If they came to church, they would not know when to stand up, when to sit down, or when to kneel. They obviously could not afford to rent a pew and they were not literate enough to navigate their way through the *Book of Common Prayer*. How could such people become Christians?

John Wesley and his compatriots, however, raised up an apostolic order within the Church of England that came to be known as Methodism. The Methodist societies, classes, and people launched an apostolic movement among the very population that establishment church leaders considered unreachable. And Wesley reflected that "religion must NOT go from the greatest to the least, or the power would appear to be of men." By reaching an allegedly hopeless population, Wesley believed his movement was dramatizing "the wideness of God's mercy."

For decades in the nineteenth century, Methodism in India cooperated with the trickle-down model of Christian mission. Methodist missionaries mainly engaged the Brahmins and other educated elites; they believed that if they first won the intelligentsia, the movement would trickle down to the masses. The theory seemed logical and its implementation put missionaries in touch with their educational peers with whom they related most naturally; but Christianity experienced little advancement by that strategy. In the late nineteenth and early twentieth centuries, however, a Christian movement broke out among some of the lowest "untouchable" castes. But, Western church leaders reasoned, how valid could this mass movement be, considering the people it was reaching? They commissioned J. Waskom Pickett to assemble a team to engage in three years of field research in this movement. Pickett's *Christian Mass Movements in India* strongly validated the movement's authenticity, strength, and miracles. He learned that we must "never judge Christianity by the people it reaches, but by the people it produces."

In recent history, one of our doctoral students in mission at Asbury has led such a movement. Vasile Talos was the leader of the Baptist Church in Romania for ten years, in a period that included the late struggles under Communism as well as the first years following Communism's demise. He enrolled in a doctoral program. One day, while reading for History of Mission in a carrel in our library, a thought occurred to him: *The Gypsies matter to God.* To some degree, Vasile confesses that he had shared Europe's wide prejudice toward the Gypsies (also known as the Roma) and Europe's assumption that Gypsies were hopeless. When he returned home, he sold his denomination on a mission to Gypsies. Today, there are more than 100 Gypsy Baptist congregations in Romania. Many cultural Romanians have observed changed lives and changed neighborhoods, and have been attracted to a church that cares enough and dares enough to serve Gypsies. By reaching Gypsies, Romania's Baptists have reached more cultural Romanians as well.

The conversion of "unlikely" people does *not* catalyze *all* of the "regular" people into receptivity. For instance, I have interviewed people in Romania who felt *less* receptive toward the Baptists now that they reach Gypsies. But some, often many, are catalyzed into seekers, and these are typically the "regular" people who'd be most useful to the Christian movement—people less inhibited and less inclined to cling to any status attached to class or ethnicity, with more altruistic personalities, who'd be more inclined to give themselves in kingdom service.

Introducing Proliferation Growth

If catalytic growth refers to a quality (as does internal growth) and is an infectious *dynamic* that we can often observe in growing Christian movements, then proliferation growth, like extension growth, refers to the *structural* innovations we typically observe in Christian movements. I am not using the term merely in the sense of the increase or multiplication of something; for example, in geopolitics we refer to "nuclear proliferation." I am using "proliferation," metaphorically, from the term's use in botany. Much of plant life obviously grows by scattering seeds near (extension growth) and far (bridging growth). Furthermore, some young plants often grow (expansion growth) in a way that is comparable to that of a young cat that grows but remains recognizably the same cat; so also a year later one can tell that a palm tree is the same palm tree one observed last year, only bigger.

Some plants, however, also grow by proliferation. For instance, some growing trees produce new trunks as well as new limbs, branches, twigs, and leaves, and they can thereby so proliferate that the mature plant may not particularly resemble the same plant when it was much younger. A tree might even extend its root system for many yards and, finding water and fertile soil, emerge vertically once again into the sun, appearing as a solitary young tree; you'd have to dig to perceive that it is an extension of the first tree. Most animals, including humans, can do nothing like this. We adult humans still have the same number of muscles, arms, and other body parts we had at birth.

But some plants grow through proliferation, and much of such a plant's growth comes through, and not without, the changes that proliferation brings about. I am told that if you plant Bermuda grass, asparagus, or bamboo, its subterranean spread over time will be so extensive that you cannot later get rid of it! I am told that if a branch of a willow tree barely touches the water of a nearby pond or lake, it will send down from the branch a new root system, which will then spread and apparently send up new young trees. My students from India tell me that their subcontinent's banyan tree grows extensively like this; plant one banyan tree in a pond and, in time, its spreading root system produces what looks like a thicket of trees. Aspen trees are the undisputed proliferation champions. One aspen tree in Utah covers 103 acres; it is the world's largest organism. The plant world sometimes exhibits proliferation growth.

We first observed the need for such a category when we saw local churches starting alternative congregations within the existing church—*not* merely like a second identical worship service more or less for the same people, but alternative congregations with their own leaders, liturgy, music, links, language, and life beyond the worship service. In the United States, we observed churches starting "contemporary" congregations to reach the baby-boom generation who, in significant numbers, could not relate to the traditional 11:00 congregation. Later, congregations emerged to reach and serve postmodern Generation X people; and then congregations surfaced for Generation Y.

Then some churches started proliferating congregations to serve people with different schedules, temperaments, or aesthetic scripting. At this writing, for instance, Hollywood's First Presbyterian Church features four Sunday congregations: a "contemplative service" meets at 8:30 in the church's chapel; a "classic service" meets at 9:30 in the sanctuary; a "CUE (contemporary urban experience) service" meets a block away at 10:45 in a renovated warehouse; a "celebration service" meets at 11:00 in the sanctuary. Again, in Jim Jackson's years as senior pastor of Chapelwood United Methodist Church in Houston, the church has transitioned from two services averaging a total of 900 people per Sunday to "a congregation of congregations" now involving more than 3000 people per weekend in one of seven distinct congregations. Saint Luke's United Methodist Church in Indianapolis involves about 3,000 people per weekend in one of ten congregations—including a Taizé congregation.

Other churches are proliferating campuses to serve people in different regions of their metropolitan area. For example, Willow Creek Community Church, in addition to featuring seeker services and Gen X services each weekend and midweek "new community" (believers) services, has planted satellite campuses in Wheaton, North Shore, McHenry County, and Chicago; each campus has its own ministries, small groups network, campus pastor, staff, and live worship, while presentations from the original South Barrington campus are videocast to the satellite congregations.

Meanwhile, churches from Singapore to Hong Kong to Kuala Lumpur are "doing church" in a half-dozen or more languages. Churches in Romania provide alternative congregations for Gypsies and other congregations for people who are deaf. Increasing numbers of churches in western Europe and North America now feature congregations of and for people who are homeless, street children, people in recovery, ex-prisoners and their families, and a range of immigrant peoples.

We have observed the most audacious expression of this principle in the proliferation of outreach ministries. Once upon a time, not so long ago, almost all churches offered pre-Christian people two options: church and Sunday school. These were the two "front doors" that were supposed to attract, welcome, and include *all* seekers. In many churches today, however, more people are primarily being reached through the proliferation of "side door" outreach ministries to an incredible range of populations—including recovery ministries for people with addictions and support groups for a range of hurting and struggling people, as well as ministries with people who are homeless; street children; single moms and single dads, and their children; people with a mental illness; immigrants; older adults; prisoners and their families; people with disabilities; people who are blind or deaf or illiterate; people needing to learn English as a second language; and many others. I am told that First Assembly of God, Phoenix, became the most rapidly growing church of its denomination through more than 200 outreach ministries.

Outreach ministries are virtually always ministries of the laity. Indeed, most outreach ministries are invented by entrepreneurial laypeople who are concerned for some specific population. Most outreach ministries become effective through a basic marketing strategy: (a) the leaders identify an underserved population; (b) they work to understand the target population; (c) they develop one or more ministries to engage them; and (d) they interpret and offer the ministry to the target population. Many outreach ministries catalyze interest in people beyond—sometimes far beyond—the target population. For instance, when a church helps a gambling addict find freedom, it may reach the addict's whole family; and when a church serves people who are deaf, it reaches those people and their families, as well as the many people who are magnetically attracted to a church that cares enough to serve the Deaf.

The proliferation growth described in the preceding paragraphs cannot be adequately understood as extension growth. The churches that multiply congregations and outreach ministries are not usually buying land, assigning a church-planting pastor or team, or engaging in most of the other activities usually associated with church planting, although the satellite congregations may resemble church plants. For instance, the twelve congregations of Wesley Methodist Church, Singapore, (four "traditional," four "prayer and praise," one Filipino, one Mandarin, and two Korean congregations) are all congregations of Wesley Church—one church with many congregations, and each congregation with many classes, groups, and ministries. Such churches grow *as* they "proliferate" groups, congregations, ministries, and outreach ministries. The body of Christ grows like a tree!

In local Christian movements, as they are fueled by the proliferation of structures and ministries, evangelistic contacts also proliferate. Leaders and other people involved in new congregations, groups, and ministries invite many people to join them. More of the active Christians, with many of the new Christians, initiate ministry and conversation with pre-Christian people. More pre-Christian people are contacted and invited, and more Christians contact more pre-Christian people more times. This is significant for no more profound reason than most people do not respond the first time they are contacted or invited; many pre-Christian people respond only after they are contacted and invited several times or more.

Proliferation growth often overlaps with McGavran's four types. Just like a tree growing through proliferation must be growing more roots and deeper roots, so growing churches must experience greater internal growth—and they experience internal growth through, and not without, proliferation. For instance, they proliferate many opportunities and types of opportunities for people to study the Scriptures. One church, for example, features Bible study in many Sunday school classes while also featuring several types of Bible study groups and a churchwide study on the book the pastor is preaching from this month or season. Simultaneously, the church challenges people with high-expectation studies like the Bethel Bible Series AND the DISCIPLE Bible Study while also hosting the extension campus of a regional seminary that makes its courses in Scripture available to church members. Likewise, many churches take a redundant approach to spiritual formation. The opportunities proliferate far beyond the Wednesday-night prayer meeting and the one page of *The Upper Room* devotional guide for the day; they may include a range of options from a dozen weekly prayer meetings to "soul friends," spiritual formation groups, retreats, pilgrimages, eucharistic services, and intercession ministries.

Expansion growth happens much more often through proliferation than without it. When traditional church leaders wish for growth, their hope does not usually range beyond, for example, seeing more people in the one eleven o'clock congregation or seeing more children in the one Sunday school class for second graders. *If* the church experiences significant new growth, however, most of the growth will be achieved through the proliferation of multiple worshiping congregations, Sunday school classes, small groups, large groups, ministries, outreach ministries, congregations, and perhaps even multiple campuses.

Extension growth is, increasingly, incorporating a proliferation paradigm. More and more new churches plan, from the beginning, to reach many people through many groups, ministries, and congregations.

Furthermore, bridging growth is becoming more proliferative. More and more churches support the denomination's missionaries, while also supporting parachurch missionaries and their church's own missionaries while also deploying many teams of laypeople in short-term mission experiences each year.

Proliferation growth represents a paradigm that is not already present and operative in the minds of most traditional church leaders. We have already seen, for instance, that local church leaders who *want* growth usually think only of making their one congregation larger. Unlike the tree, which is genetically encoded to proliferate, with an inborn capacity to extend its roots toward moist soil or to adapt to climate change, proliferation does not come naturally to humans and their organizations. The capacity to grow through proliferation comes through learning; any specific expression of the principle, like a new congregation for the Deaf, must first be imagined, planned, resourced, marketed, staffed, and managed—and then be improved through reflection upon experience. You have to imagine it and manage it to achieve it.

Furthermore, most traditional church leaders operate with the value of efficiency strongly in mind, and when efficiency occupies a leader's mind, it crowds out proliferation. For example, "Why start another congregation? The one eleven o'clock service we have now is not full!" When we implement proliferation growth, however, it sets up shop on both sides of efficiency. On one side, it is enormously more efficient than a traditional one-congregation church; with multiple congregations sharing the same space and staff, and multiple outreach ministries housed in or moving out from the same space, the church is maximizing its facilities and personnel much more efficiently and cost-effectively than we observe in traditional churches. On the other side of efficiency, a proliferation strategy may not wait until what the church is already doing is "full," or even self-supporting; it moves toward opportunity as soon as God gives the leaders that a new group, ministry, or congregation will need.

In churches hoping to transition from tradition to mission, we typically meet one entrenched barrier to growth through proliferation. "We can't start another service. Our pastor (or staff) already feels overworked." Traditional leaders still assume that the pastor and staff are paid to do most of the ministry that matters AND that they would have to lead any and all new congregations, including ethnic-language congregations, AND that they would have to do any outreach ministries as well. Proliferation growth depends on a contrasting assumption: God wants to entrust most of the ministry that matters to laypeople whom God has gifted and called for ministry within and beyond the congregation. Contagious Christian movements are lay movements, and lay movements grow through—and not without—the proliferation of ministries. Since lay Christian movements need healthy pastors, growth may depend upon proliferating teaching pastors and other staff as needed; their focus, however, is not upon "doing ministry" as much as it is upon "leading and feeding" everyone else's ministry!

The proliferation analogy, drawn from botany, can suggest some of the interventions in which leaders can engage to increase a church's health, reach, and growth. For instance, a church could discern in every season where in the wider community it is called to "branch out," extend roots, or scatter seeds. Again, the leaders may even identify the branches and limbs that are dying or no longer bearing fruit and prune them to send energy to other parts of the tree that can have a more reproductive future. Leaders can even choose to prune some healthy lower limbs in order to redirect growth upward and attain the desired vision!

Proliferation growth is a new paradigm for understanding, beyond McGavran's four types, many—but not all—of the ways the church grows. When, for example, a church's Korean congregation votes to leave, acquire land, relocate, and change their name, is that proliferation growth, extension growth, or bridging growth? This promising classification will not account for all of the ways the church grows; nor will catalytic growth; but they nevertheless provide two new paradigms that will inform the growth of churches in many new ways.

◆　　　◆　　　◆　　　◆

The two case studies that follow reflect two Christian movements, both in North America, that are as different from each other as one could imagine. They will help us see the catalytic and proliferation dynamics from two contrasting perspectives.

The Case of Redeemer Presbyterian Church, Manhattan

In North America, Protestant Christianity has often failed to engage urban populations, and Protestant people have often preferred the suburbs, the towns, and the hinterlands to the complexity, the challenges, the crime, and the costs of an urban presence. We Protestant Christians never officially announced that the city's peoples were "impossible" to reach, but we seem to have assumed something like that.

The United Methodist Church's unspoken outlook is typical. The UMC covers the national landscape and the distribution of its churches looks impressive on a map. Virtually every town, village, and hamlet has a Methodist church—an achievement that commemorates Methodism's nineteenth-century strategy to plant churches for the country's westward migrating populations and to provide a pastor and a church to the thousands of settlements that were scattered almost everywhere.

But national Methodism, once American Christianity's strategic pioneer, has never adequately adjusted to the nation's changing demographics. In the late nineteenth century, the population of the United States was less than 20 percent urban and more than 80 percent rural; it made strategic sense to serve the people as they were then scattered across the land. Today, however, the population is more than 80 percent urban and less than 20 percent rural, but the denomination still deploys its clergy, and maintains most of its churches, where most of the people used to be. A study of specific Methodist districts is especially revealing. The Bakersfield, California, district and the Los Angeles district cover comparably sized areas on California's map, and each district has about the same number of churches and clergy. The Los Angeles district, however, has at least 20 times the number of people as the Bakersfield district. Across the country, United Methodism has a church for every 1,000 to 2,000 people in most of the towns, villages, and countryside, and a church for every 20,000 to 40,000 in most of the cities. In the Manhattan borough of New York City, a Google search revealed that nine United Methodist churches now serve a population of 1,600,000.

◆   ◆   ◆   ◆

Occasionally, a would-be Protestant movement has targeted a city. Dwight L. Moody once observed, "Whoever wins the city, wins." After 20 years of itinerant evangelism, Moody gave the rest of his life to reaching one city: Chicago. Moody Church and Moody Bible Institute still remind us that Moody dreamed in the tradition of the apostles. Today, a century after Moody, Tim Keller and the people of Redeemer Presbyterian Church, Manhattan, are demonstrating that such cities are not as hopeless as most Protestant leaders have assumed.

Timothy Keller was teaching at Westminster Theological Seminary in Philadelphia when, in the late 1980s, a group of concerned evangelicals prevailed upon him to lead a new church plant in Manhattan. Manhattan was and is the financial, business, cultural, and communications center for the nation and beyond. Keller and his core leaders developed a profile of the people the new church was called to reach. They were (and are): extremely bright and experts in their fields or aspired to be; had years of counseling behind them and tended to think in psychological terms; were extremely sexually active; were absorbed in their careers, with most of their relationships in their job field; had a liberal social conscience; were commitment phobic and highly private and individualistic; were very lonely; experienced constant and numerous tumultuous transitions; were very secular but had tried at least two or three different religious systems already; and were very mistrustful of organized religion and evangelical Christianity in particular.[18]

The new church would *target* those very populations, as well as students, graduate students, and professors from the borough's higher education institutions. Redeemer's leaders experienced one pleasant discovery. Most New Yorkers recognized the "Presbyterian" and "Episcopalian" brands, and most other Protestant names connoted "cult," so the new church would feature its historic roots and identity. A prominent feature of Redeemer's vision was to produce a generation of *Christian* artists, musicians, composers, playwrights, executives, and so on. Today, several hundred members are involved in music, dance, opera, and other arts.

Redeemer Church began worship on Sunday evenings in 1989 in a rented space in a Seventh Day Adventist church. They began as a church plant of the Presbyterian Church in America (PCA). (Redeemer's congregations have been meeting in rented space, such as the Hunter College auditorium, ever since. The church's office, however, has a Broadway address!) The movement was launched in the service of an audacious vision statement (periodically revised). The current version announces that

21

Redeemer Presbyterian Church's vision is "to build a great city for all people—through a gospel movement that brings personal conversion, community formation, social justice, and cultural renewal to New York and, through it, to the world."

Within a year, average attendance grew from 50 to 400; in three years it grew to 1,000. Today, about 6,000 people celebrate each Sunday in one or another of Redeemer's five congregations strategically scattered across Manhattan Island. Redeemer is a high-expectation church, so attendance is at least triple the membership. People become new members only after completing a course and an interview, and committing to lay ministry, small group life, theological and spiritual formation, and to live as Christians in their vocation. Even so, the church now receives more than 150 new members into membership per year; half are new Christians. Keller insists, "The purpose is not to just increase the tribe, but to change the city."

From the beginning, Redeemer Church has purposed to be a "church planting movement." Each year their Church Planting Center trains 20 to 30 pastors to plant churches that reflect Redeemer's vision and philosophy.[19] The Center has facilitated many church plants (PCA and churches of other denominations), including 50 churches across metropolitan New York City, with another 80 plants in many other cities in the United States, such as Boston, Washington, and San Francisco, and in major cities on other continents, such as Berlin, London, and Amsterdam. The Center's leaders report that the main lessons for church planters take redundant teaching and experiences: would-be urban pastors need to learn to love and understand the city, and to assume *no* prior Christian knowledge in the minds of pre-Christian people; and they need to experience the profound paradigm shift involved in moving from moralism to grace in their preaching, teaching, and witness.

Redeemer's leaders discovered early that reaching the target population of literate, educated, professional people from the city's financial, cultural, and media sectors typically involves a lengthy process. Many people begin the pilgrimage toward faith knowing virtually nothing or "knowing" some things they will have to unlearn. A church has to begin "farther back" with these people, and they usually become Christians by the cumulative effect of many experiences and decisions, not one big experience or decision. With these populations, the ministry of apologetics is often necessary. For years, Redeemer relied on apologetics classics like C. S. Lewis's *Mere Christianity*, but since some of the questions and issues have changed over time, Redeemer evolved its own curriculum, which is reflected in Keller's recent book, *The Reason for God*.[20] The church also discovered that the knowledge of even basic Christianity is so deficient in the minds of seekers, new Christians, and even transferring Christians that they require their Christian Foundations course for all new members. The heart of that curriculum is now reflected in Keller's *The Prodigal God*.[21]

With the educational background of Redeemer's target population, the church's indigenous approach to pedagogy takes the form of seminars. The peoples' cognitive journey begins with the School of Gospel Foundations. The journey is not entirely intellectual, however. Redeemer teaches people, from the beginning, that Christianity is "a religion of the heart," and the focus is frequently on spiritual formation, life commitment, one's vocation in the world, and especially the formation of a Christian worldview. The church offers an extensive range of elective seminars in Scripture, church history, and theology—all with application to the people of God's life in the world. The church schedules frequent seminars and events for people in the arts and other sectors.

Redeemer Church's leaders believe that "God made us for community," and Redeemer's people have experienced that life in community is indispensable to living as Christians, especially in the city. Redeemer's people know one another and engage in ministry with one another in "fellowship groups." The leaders decided early that most of the ministry to individuals would take place in small groups. They planned for nearly every member, and many attendees and non-Christians, to be in ministry with one another in groups. Today, six to twelve people meet weekly or biweekly in typical fellowship groups in homes and offices across the city. Many groups also have a service project. Although Redeemer Church has not yet reached the goal of every member being involved in a fellowship group, most of the members and many others meet in one of more than 200 fellowship groups.[22]

Tim Keller explains that Redeemer Presbyterian Church was started not to primarily serve Christians but rather for the sake of pre-Christian people and for the sake of the city. From the beginning they hoped to be more of a gospel movement than another institutional church, and they planned to be a church of multiple congregations that would plant many city churches. Though people in many city churches seem to loathe the city, Redeemer's founding members believed that a city needs more churches that love the city. They believed that the city needs culture-friendly churches that engage in holistic ministry, including social concerns. In New York City, being "culture friendly" necessarily means engaging multiple cultures, especially underreached cultures. So, of Redeemer's five congregations, one will find a jazz congregation and another that features classical Christian music!

Redeemer Presbyterian Church provides a hopeful model for many churches, in part because it models how church leaders deal with complexity—not by denying it or oversimplifying it, but by working through the complexity to arrive at the relative simplicity that awaits truth-seekers on the other side. You engage the people by understanding their culture, issues, and needs. Communicating the gospel to secular city people is a complex process because they know so little, they are unfamiliar with many of the Christian faith's most treasured words and symbols, and especially because "people do not realize that their deepest desires often do not match up with their deepest needs." Most people, Keller observes, are "asking God to get us over that little hump so we can save ourselves. It doesn't occur to us that we're looking for something besides Jesus to save us." Keller coaches church leaders to abandon the quest for power. "If you seek to serve people more than to gain power, you will not only serve people, you will gain influence."[23]

Is Redeemer's growth partly accounted for by the metaphor of catalytic growth? Yes, as they have targeted and reached the kind of educated "up and outers" that most churches do not even attempt to reach, many other people have become more responsive to the church's appeal and the gospel's power. Admittedly, Redeemer Church does not reach many people who are illiterate, addicted, or people who speak ethnic-minority languages, but some of Redeemer's church plants do. Their achievement reminds us that in heterogeneous cities there is a limit to the population range that one church can reach and serve; but there may be no known limit to the range of people that the church can reach through the proliferation of congregations and ministries.

Is Redeemer's growth partly accounted for as proliferation growth? Yes, there is no reason to believe that Redeemer could be reaching nearly as many people through one congregation in one location as they are reaching through five congregations in several locations. Furthermore, their many lay-led outreach ministries validate the concept. Redeemer's network of fellowship groups comes up somewhat short because the groups are all essentially the same; they have *multiplied* similar fellowship groups, but they have not *proliferated* the wide range of different kinds of groups (such as support groups, recovery groups, mission groups, and others) that are possible in cities today, although some of their church plants feature other kinds of groups. Redeemer's virtually unparalleled commitment to church planting, including the planting of many different kinds of churches, serves as a prototype of proliferation growth.

The Case of the Inuit Christian Movement, Northern Canada

The promotional ministries of Roger Armbruster (www.canadaawakening.com) and the opening segment of the *Transformations II* video (www.sentinelgroup.org) have alerted much of the Christian world to a Christian movement among the Inuit aboriginal peoples of the North American Arctic. The Inuit people (sometimes called "Eskimos") number about 125,000 individuals scattered in seacoast villages of 300 to 2,000 people across much of Arctic Canada and Alaska, with more Inuit in Greenland and Russia. The first known seed for their movement was planted in the late nineteenth century when an Inuit shaman, Angwatisiak, learned through a vision that a man would one day bring news of a son of God to the Inuit.

In the late 1920s, when the Church Mission Society of the Church of England sent Canon John Turner to Pond Inlet, Canada, as the first missionary to an Inuit people, Angwatisiak's grandsons recognized the missionary from what they recalled of their grandfather's prophecy! In the decade before his untimely death, Turner built a solid church in Pond Inlet while planting seeds in neighboring Arctic communities. In time, the Church Mission Society sent missionaries and planted churches in most of the communities of Arctic Canada. Through the later itineration, by plane, of the Reverend John Spillenaar in the late 1960s through the 1980s, the Full Gospel Church also planted many Inuit congregations. Today, David Ellyatt has succeeded Spillenaar in leading the Arctic Missions agency (www.arcticmissions.com), which takes teams of laity into Arctic communities each summer to join indigenous Christians in building or expanding church facilities.

The spread of Christianity, in both the Anglican and the Full Gospel traditions, proceeded slowly until February of 1996 when a gospel movement broke out in Pond Inlet (and, rather concurrently, in several other communities) and spread within months to many Inuit communities. In September 2003, I attended a conference of more than 300 Inuit Christian people from 35 communities across Arctic Canada, which met in Baker Lake, Nunavut Territory, Canada. One purpose of my visit was to test the validity and usefulness of my two paradigms (catalytic and proliferation) through observations in Baker Lake and through interviews with church leaders and converts from other communities. Both paradigms were confirmed, but from different directions.

◆   ◆   ◆   ◆

The Inuit Christian movement fits the catalytic growth paradigm profoundly. Indeed, when the movement broke out in Pond Inlet, the news spread to other communities; when Pond Inlet Christians visited and spoke in other communities, this catalyzed interest and outreach in about 18 Inuit communities across northern Canada. Many non-Inuit Canadians regard the Inuit people like many Europeans regard Gypsies, so news of an awakening among this allegedly "hopeless" population has triggered a wider curiosity.

In Pond Inlet, at least 80 percent of the community's people were addicted to a range of substances from alcohol to gasoline fumes; crime, child abuse, spousal abuse, depression, and suicide scourged the town. In February 1996, three addicts experienced faith and the church served as their de facto recovery community. The church reached out to other addicts, who also responded, and to their families and friends. When the sober pre-Christian townspeople saw these "hopeless" people leading new lives, many of them sought the grace that has that kind of power. I was told that in more than a dozen of Canada's Arctic communities the transformative conversions of addicts has catalyzed the growth of at least some of the churches.

I was told that many of these Arctic communities have been lawless, like the old American West. Wild, violence-prone young men who often abuse women and children, and who fight and even kill, have threatened the peace of many of these communities. One young man, who spoke one evening at the Baker Lake conference, reported that he had been "the worst" such man in his town; when he accepted Christ and a new life, several of his peers followed, and other people were so impressed by these obvious miracles in their midst that they responded. Most of these Arctic communities, people reported, are much safer and more peaceful since the awakening hit town!

Suicide can become epidemic in Arctic communities; some communities lose 1 percent of their people to suicide in a given year. The mayor of one community, once a nominal Christian and a competent leader, reported that his community averaged a suicide a month for two years. He tried everything he had learned in leadership, management, and human relations training, but the monthly suicides continued "like clockwork." In desperation, he confessed to his church one Sunday morning that he needed the Holy Spirit's power; if he needed the Holy Spirit, perhaps other people in the church did too. The change in him catalyzed a revival in the town, and the suicide epidemic ceased.

I interviewed five pre-Christian Anglos who worked in Baker Lake in jobs such as teaching, plumbing, and wildlife preservation. Four of the five said they were deeply moved by the changes they had observed in some of the Inuit people who had become

Christians in Baker Lake. Two accepted my invitation to attend one or more of the evening services of the conference; they were moved by what they witnessed, and one has since joined the Anglican church in Baker Lake as a new Christian. On the way home, I interviewed five Anglos in the Winnipeg airport and hotel who had heard of the Inuit awakening and they were very interested in my firsthand report; they responded with exclamations like, "Who would have ever thought it possible?"

The conversion of "unlikely" people does *not* catalyze *all* of the "regular" people into receptivity. For instance, I have interviewed people in Romania who felt *less* receptive toward the Baptists now that they serve Gypsies, and one person in Winnipeg's airport said that she would "have nothing to do with a religion that welcomes people like them Eskimos." But some people are catalyzed into greater receptivity and these are typically the "regular" people who'd be most useful to the Christian movement—people less inclined to define themselves by any status attached to class or ethnicity and more inclined to self-giving.

◆　　◆　　◆　　◆

Whereas the catalytic growth category seemed validated by these and other cases in the Inuit Christian movement, I found much less evidence for the proliferation growth theory. People from several communities reported that their awakening empowered the church members for more outreach to more people more times. One woman reflected that she'd only been invited to a church twice in her earlier life. "Now, suddenly, many friends were inviting me and inviting me again!" But few churches reported new groups, few reported new ministries, and no one reported new congregations; they still had one worshiping congregation per Sunday.

One day, when I interviewed people in Baker Lake's general store, three people said they were or had been interested in being involved in one of Baker Lake's four churches, but when they visited "there was no room" for them, or they heard through the grapevine that "the church is full now; no more room." People attending the conference from at least eight churches reported that their churches had grown a lot, that their churches were now full most Sundays, and that their churches were no longer growing as much or at all. Then it occurred to me that *this* is a probable reason many of these local Christian movements, which exploded in the late 1990s, have plateaued in more recent years. As I visited Baker Lake's four churches, I estimated their total seating capacity to be less than 400. So if *every* church were full in its one service each Sunday, there would be no room for at least 1,400 of Baker Lake's 1,800 people.

Many church leaders would suggest that if these Inuit Christian movements are to continue growing, they will have to plant more churches; I was told, however, that with the need to import most materials and specialized labor, the cost of building more churches is more than prohibitive and that the Arctic Missions agency cannot build or expand enough one-service-per-Sunday churches to keep up with the growth that is possible. In Inuit communities, therefore, proliferation growth is a much more feasible opportunity than extension growth. With the Inuits' distinctive tribal community ethos, however, I was told that *no* churches have a precedent for adding a second congregation: "We love for everyone to be together." (Terry LeBlanc, who works with many North American tribal peoples and churches, recalls no Native church in North America that has more than one congregation.)

Like many churches in many cultures that are used to "the one worship service," Inuit Christianity's leaders will have to weigh the trade-offs and consider the proliferation paradigm. (I am told that some traditional communities in other cultural regions of the earth have "sandwiched" a lengthy fellowship period for everyone between the first and second service. So they added a congregation AND scheduled an experience for "everyone to be together.") If they do *not* proliferate congregations within their churches, many receptive people will not be reached, the movement will lose momentum, the churches will have missed the day of many people's visitation, and their glorious movement will become a glorious memory.

CHAPTER TWO

WHAT KIND OF CHURCH REACHES PRE-CHRISTIAN PEOPLE?

One spring, in the early 1980s, the great American folk preacher and storyteller Tex Evans was to preach one Sunday at a Methodist church in Maryland. The special occasion was the two hundredth anniversary of the day when Methodism's apostle to America, Francis Asbury, crossed the nearby river on horseback to preach to the gathered townspeople and plant a new Methodist church. Before the service, several men strolled with Tex the fifty yards to the river that Asbury and his horse once crossed. One man reported, "The rains had been heavy that spring. The river was swollen and raging; it was perilous to cross it. Do you want us to tell you how Asbury and his horse came across the river?" Tex reflected and said, "No. I want you to tell me *why* he crossed it!"

The men could not tell him. They had no idea, no clue. Evans scrapped his planned address, scribbled some notes on a card, and in his sermon explained to the people what it is in Christianity's good news and in the experience of its truth and power that would compel someone to bring the good news, at personal risk, to people. The pathology that Evans discovered in a church in Maryland was not an isolated problem. Most churches in North America and Europe, and many churches on all of the other continents, are afflicted with amnesia. They no longer remember who they are; they have forgotten their main business. As Paul Little once observed, "Most churches are not fishers of men; they are keepers of the aquarium!" Let's view such churches and another kind of church through the telescope of history.

◆　　◆　　◆　　◆

The people of the first-century Christian movement understood that they were the "new Israel" commissioned by the risen Lord and empowered by the Holy Spirit to bless the earth's peoples and to make Christ-followers among all peoples. The movement was *ekklesia*—they were "called out" from the world to be the new people of God. The movement was also an *apostolate*—they were "sent out" into the world to communicate the gospel of reconciliation with God and a new life in service to the will of God on earth. Christ's offer was intended for all people and peoples. Our forebears knew they were "ambassadors for Christ" through whom God would invite all people to join with Christ and his one, holy, catholic, and apostolic church.

Early Christians knew that *this* mission was their main business; if they failed God here, they failed God—regardless of whether they'd attended church, said their daily prayers, and lived moral lives. They comprehended the perspective later stated by C. S. Lewis: "The Church exists for nothing else but to draw men into Christ, to make them little Christs. If they are not doing that, all the cathedrals, clergy, missions,

29

sermons, even the Bible itself, are simply a waste of time. God became Man for no other purpose. It is even doubtful, you know, whether the whole universe was created for any other purpose."[1]

If Lewis was right, most churches today, like that church in Maryland, are "a waste of time"; they major on the minors. Most church members attend the kind of church that John Wesley once dreaded—a church with "the form of religion, but without the power." The typical church seldom experiences new people entering its ranks who are discovering new life. In the United States, for instance, Grace Reese recently completed a four-year Lilly Foundation study of *how* mainline churches do evangelism—*when* they do it. Reese identified 30,000 churches in six denominations and decided to study the churches that had received at least five new converts "from the world" per year for three successive years. To her astonishment, she discovered that only about 150 of the 30,000 churches attained this standard. Only one-half of one percent of the churches had a notable apostolic track record.[2] Many other studies have reported that 1 percent or less of Western churches experience much conversion growth from the world. (Even in the nations where Christianity now grows most, more than 80 percent of the growth comes from less than 20 percent of the churches.)

The small minority of the churches that reach pre-Christian people *should* be of interest to the other 99 percent. I have studied many such churches. The leaders of stagnant churches have usually heard of these alternative churches and they assume they understand them, but these churches do *not* usually fit the stereotype that other churches often have of them! It might be useful to know what all or most of them have in common and how they "do church," which other churches could learn from. For years, I have asked questions like: (a) What do they *know* that other churches do not know? (b) What do they *do* that other churches do not do? (c) When they do things that other churches also do, *how* do they do them differently? I have gained many insights from asking those three questions regarding the knowledge, practice, and style of apostolic congregations.[3]

When you study growing churches worldwide, you observe that the contexts of churches vary so enormously—from the Arctic to the equator, from the villages to the cities, in so many different historical and cultural conditions—that you might guess that growing churches, globally, have *nothing* in common. In chapter 1, for example, we looked at the continentwide Christian movement in Inuit villages across Canada's vast Arctic region and the growth of Redeemer Presbyterian Church among financial, music, theater, arts, and student populations of Manhattan. From just those two cases, you'd think that almost nothing is the same (except maybe for the Lord's Prayer and the Apostles' Creed).

Deeper analysis and reflection reveal, however, a number of principles that they and all or most apostolic congregations follow in common. The principles are important because they help explain how such churches prepare their people for ministry and outreach, AND how they help seekers become meaningfully involved and to discover grace. The principles are also important because, while a few pioneering churches discover and model the principles, all other churches can choose to adopt (or adapt) the principles to fit their opportunity.

◆   ◆   ◆   ◆

Cultural Relevance

We begin with the most established principle of mission studies—the principle of "indigenous" Christianity. Churches that are culturally relevant to the population they want to reach tend to reach them in much greater numbers than churches that use culturally alien forms in worship and ministry. Although this policy was decided at the Jerusalem Council (reported in Acts 15), Christianity has had to relearn this lesson over and over again. The forms through which *we* made sense of Christianity make so much sense to *us* that we assume those forms would be best for everybody. We *may* see the need to do ministry in the target population's language (though most churches in the United States seem stuck on the idea of English for everyone). It takes a while to realize (as Edward T. Hall taught us) that culture is "the silent language"; the communication of meaning is blocked by, or leaks out through, the many ways we communicate, consciously or unconsciously. So effective churches adapt to the target population's style, language, music, and aesthetics because each people's culture is the most effective medium of God's revelation to them.

Emotional Relevance

If cultural relevance is our most established principle, emotional relevance is, academically, our least established principle—although apostolic congregations frequently practice it intuitively without knowing what to call it. The Enlightenment's theory of human nature perceived people as essentially rational creatures. It was believed that the human capacity for reason separated people from the beasts of the forests and jungles. From our more primitive and less enlightened forebears, we do experience emotions, and emotions do sometimes get in the way or even become dysfunctional, so we all need to be educated out of our residual feelings and into the rational life of the mind.

The Enlightenment was wrong by about 180 degrees. Human beings are essentially *emotional* creatures who are sometimes capable of thinking! But even when we think, our background emotional state influences what we think about, and our more active feelings influence how we think about it. The Romantic Era once challenged the Enlightenment's theory of human nature, and Jonathan Edwards and John Wesley were once clear about the role of "religious affections" in Christian experience.

Today's leaders of the most effective churches also know this. They know that many people's souls are crippled by stress and by an out-of-control emotional war within, and that they often feel that "no one knows how I feel, not even God." Leaders of the most effective churches take this seriously, and they know that authentic conversion involves experiencing a new emotional world with specific emotions like joy, peace, and gratitude, which people had not known before. Effective churches begin with people where they are; they consider people's emotional agendas and their struggle for emotional freedom; and they adapt their music, preaching, teaching, praying, counseling, and pastoral care to the emotional needs and aspirations of people.

Small Groups

The principle of small groups in apostolic congregations is the most widely known principle. Indeed, almost every church has small groups within its life—often several

31

types of small groups. Can anything new be said about small groups? Yes, so much so that the cumulative case for taking them even more seriously is compelling.

For instance, the initial reason they are prominent in the more apostolic churches is because in small groups of any type (such as study groups, interest groups, support groups, service groups, and recovery groups), the group is effective *if* the people are in ministry with one another. When they pull for one another, intercede for one another, rejoice and weep with one another, hold one another accountable, and experience the power of *koinonia* fellowship and what Paul called being "members of one another" (Ephesians 4:25), then all the people are better cared for than in the traditional church, where one ordained chaplain tries to do all the shepherding.

Other important things happen in small group life, but not usually outside it. For instance, in small groups people discern one another's gifts for ministry. In small groups, people gain experience in lay ministry and are more likely to minister to people outside the group and outside the church. In small groups with an "empty chair" that they fill with a seeker every six months, small groups reach people. In many churches, the groups, rather than a worship service, are the initial ports of entry for far more seekers. In small groups with a seeker or two in their fellowship, Christians gain experience in the ministry of Christian witness and are more likely to engage in the ministry of witness outside the group and outside the church. Leaders surface in small groups. Leaders are developed in small groups. The whole church grows *as* it proliferates small groups. All of this and more is why more and more churches are becoming churches *of* small groups. This is why Bruce Larson used to say, "It is just as important to be involved in a small group as it is to believe that Jesus Christ died for your sins!"

Lay Ministries

We have paid lip service to the principle of *lay ministries* ever since Martin Luther rediscovered the doctrine of "the priesthood of all believers," but the principle has seldom been implemented. The early Christianity recorded in the New Testament was a lay movement. No one in the movement was ordained, in the sense that any tradition now means it, for the movement's first one hundred years. In time, however, most of the ministry that mattered was reassigned to priests and, later, to Protestant pastors.

Today, worldwide, wherever most of the ministry that matters is assigned to the clergy, Christianity stagnates or declines. Today, worldwide, wherever most of the ministry that matters is entrusted to laity, the church grows and is sometimes a contagious, unstoppable movement in all but impossible circumstances—such as the church's growth in China in the last thirty years.[4] The folk wisdom in our Christian traditions sometimes knows this. For instance, evangelists in the American Holiness tradition observed, "Shepherds don't make new sheep; sheep make new sheep." This wisdom does NOT suggest the elimination of ordained clergy, but it does suggest their different role. In local Christian movements, the clergy challenge and support the laity; they educate and encourage the laity; they lead and feed the laity for *their* ministry and mission.

Proliferation of Groups, Ministries, Congregations, and Leaders

Apostolic congregations reach people and grow through *proliferation*. As we saw in the previous chapter, that unusual term is borrowed from botanists, who use it to describe the way that many plants grow (such as, especially, banyan trees and aspen trees). These plants do not grow, for example, like a cat, which grows from kitten to cat while retaining the same features, the same number of limbs, and so on. When an aspen tree has grown for years, it doesn't look at all like the same tree it was years before. It has proliferated limbs, branches, twigs, leaves, and even multiple trunks for which, years earlier, there were no visual hints. One aspen tree in Utah covers 103 acres. You would have to dig to see that all the trunks are connected and part of the same organism.

Most traditional churches try to grow like a cat; they want to stay the same but get bigger. So they ask questions like, "How can we increase attendance in our one worship service?" It is not a useless question. Some growth without structural change is usually possible. But apostolic congregations typically ask a second question: "How can we grow by adding, even multiplying, small groups, large groups, congregations, ministries, and leaders, and by increasing the number of populations we serve?" Although both questions are important, traditional churches usually ask only the first; but the most growth comes by asking the second.

Social Network Outreach

Many of an apostolic congregation's people do evangelism—not so much public evangelistic campaigns or preaching one-on-one to strangers, but rather reaching out across social networks to invite and involve friends, relatives, and neighbors who are not yet disciples. Our people's social networks provide what Donald McGavran called "the bridges of God." Whereas the church teaches and encourages lay evangelism, the dynamics we have covered especially prepare the people for "gossiping the gospel." Laity are much more energized to invite their friends if their church is culturally and emotionally relevant to their friends' lives. When laity get involved in a ministry— almost *any* ministry to people—they are more likely to evangelize. And when in their small groups they gain experience in ministry with seekers and in talking about the gospel, they are primed for evangelism far beyond the group.

How the laity do evangelism is typically the ministry of conversation—two-way conversation. They engage in many conversations over time, in which they often do more listening than talking. Often they invite people to come with them to a group, a service, an outreach ministry, or perhaps an eight-week study introducing Christianity, and the conversation emerges naturally from the shared experience.

◆　　◆　　◆　　◆

Those six principles—cultural relevance, emotional relevance, small groups, lay ministries, structural proliferation, and social network evangelism—are nearly universal in the churches that grow substantially by conversion growth. Four more principles are emerging and spreading, and they contribute to the reproductivity of many churches, but they are not yet universal.

Outreach Ministries

Outreach ministries is a frontier topic for understanding the world's most reproductive churches. Once upon a time, not so long ago, we relied on two "front doors" for reaching people: the worship service and the Sunday school. Today, the most apostolic congregations reach even more people through many "side doors," such as small groups and outreach ministries. We can propose only three generalizations about outreach ministries: (1) they often take place in the community, beyond the church's campus; (2) they are usually lay led; (3) they are often lay invented.

A given outreach ministry may, of course, be found in thousands of places (such as recovery ministries), and some are adopted or adapted from other churches (such as Saddleback Church's Celebrate Recovery ministry). More often, however, entrepreneurial laypeople perceive a need, develop an innovative ministry, and mobilize other laypeople who share their passion. One example will express the spirit of many. A woman at Frazer Memorial United Methodist Church in Montgomery, Alabama, learned that when premature babies were born in Montgomery's several hospitals, the hospital and parents often could not find clothing for, say, a three-pound baby; apparently no clothing manufacturer serves that small market. The woman organized a team of women who love to sew. They now sew the booties, gowns, and caps for every premature baby born in any hospital in Montgomery. They take the clothing to the hospitals and they minister to anxious families. Although the ministry has no strings attached, many families of preemies have joined Frazer Church, some as new Christians.

Radical Outreach

Consistent with outreach ministries, many apostolic congregations engage in "radical outreach"; they reach people whom more traditional congregations seldom consider reaching, such as more marginalized, allegedly "impossible" or "hopeless" people and other populations who are not at all like "good church people." The very earliest Christian movement began this way. Jesus of Nazareth engaged a range of people that included lepers and people who were blind, deaf, possessed, or mentally ill, as well as prostitutes, tax collectors, Samaritans, Gentiles, and zealots. What did all of these groups have in common? None of these groups were permitted in the Temple. Most of the apostles continued this bold tradition, reaching "barbarian" populations (and even cannibal populations).

As in the case of the fifth-to-ninth-century Celtic Christian movement and John Wesley's eighteenth-century Methodism, this apostolic tradition has been periodically recovered. Both movements reached populations that establishment Christianity considered impossible to Christianize. Many churches today reach the "new barbarians," including the people who live on the wild side who are looking for life, but in all the wrong places. Some of them are reached, and they experience grace and obvious transformation. As other, more "normal," people observe these miracles, they become more receptive to the faith, and the Christian movement spreads.[5]

Social Conscience

Many apostolic congregations, in many lands and cultures, are experiencing and acting on a wider social conscience. For instance, in the United States, where abortion has been a social and political issue, these churches have usually been "pro-life." More recently, some have reasoned that being pro-life should mean more than being "pro-birth"! So they extend their Christian affirmation of life to include commitment to childcare, health care, gun control, peace, a healthy creation, or animal rights.

Beyond the United States, on all inhabited continents, some churches that have been reaching pre-Christian people are discovering that Christians are called to be kingdom people who work to change communities and nations. Churches that for years have dispensed medicine to sick children now also work for clean water and sanitation so there will be fewer sick children. Churches that have ministered to AIDS patients and their families now also work for the laws and lifestyle changes that will prevent many people from ever contracting AIDS. Churches that have helped poor people are now also digging wells; starting schools; pioneering cottage industries; advocating for roads, electricity, and jobs; and engaging in other interventions to help abjectly poor people reach the lowest step on the economic ladder.[6] A recent global study demonstrates that many Pentecostal churches in the branch of Christianity long considered the least socially prophetic are now socially engaged and are changing communities.[7]

In contrast to the church traditions that have championed a "social gospel" for a century or more, apostolic congregations are careful to avoid the trap of making it more "social" than "gospel," and they do not engage in social concerns *instead* of doing evangelism. Their new social involvement actually contributes to their evangelism. Their people with knowledge and passion for education, health care, or economics are now making the contribution for which God has shaped them, and they are now more likely to also evangelize. Furthermore, poor people or environmentalists now perceive that the church is on their side and they become more receptive to its message.[8] As one of many examples, Donald E. Miller and Tetsunao Yamamori cite a Pentecostal church in Caracas, Venezuela, whose "extensive network of social services . . . has fueled the growth of the congregation because of the church's reputation that it cares for people in need."[9] Furthermore, such a church's evangelism provides an ever-expanding army of disciples who follow Jesus into his world to make a difference.

World Mission Involvement

More and more churches realize that the Lord's commission extends far beyond their local church's ministry area, so they involve their people in much wider mission, usually in other cultures and often in other nations. India, for instance, is as multilingual and multicultural as all of western Europe, so it is not necessary for Indian Christians to leave their country to engage in cross-cultural mission. Today, more Indian Christian missionaries are reaching other ethnic peoples within India than ever before, and more people of their sponsoring churches become involved in short-term mission than ever before.

University Presbyterian Church, Seattle, once pioneered an extravagant approach to mission that modeled a way for many other churches.[10] For years, the church supported more than 70 missionaries AND sent out 300 or more people per year in short-term mission teams. For example, a team would spend three weeks digging wells in India or replacing a church's roof in a Guatemalan village while sharing community with the local Christians in the evenings. Senior Pastor Bruce Larson reflected that in those three weeks, "They did no harm; they did a little good; they discovered who they are; and they came back home on fire for mission!" They had acquired "missionary eyes." They now perceived *Seattle* as a mission field! The church planted several ethnic-minority-language churches in Seattle—including a Farsi-speaking Iranian Presbyterian congregation!

◆　　◆　　◆　　◆

Postscript

We might add, as a postscript, that most of the world's apostolic congregations are *high-expectation* churches; they expect much more of their people than traditional churches do. Dean M. Kelley introduced this idea in the 1970s. As a sociologist, he studied denominations that had experienced sustained growth and he wrote *Why Conservative Churches Are Growing*.[11] Alas, the publisher imposed an inaccurate title. Kelley was actually describing why "strict" or "demanding" religious traditions experience long-term growth. He observed that when traditions lower their membership standards (as American Methodism did in the early twentieth century), they may receive more members for a while, "but at the price of religious vitality" and the near certainty of long-term membership stagnation or decline.

Furthermore, Kelley observed that most religious seekers are not very sophisticated in thinking through contrasting or competing religious truth claims. So they look to see which religious group seems to believe in their message the most, to invest time and energy for it, and even to sacrifice for it. They find *that* church's message the most credible.

Kelley's thesis has experienced some evolution in a generation. Most scholars now agree that, long term, the churches that expect much from their people grow much more long term than churches that only expect church attendance and little more. Kelley observed that his "strict" churches expected their people to comply with the movement's rules and norms—such as a prohibition against drinking alcohol. We now see that, while such disciplines are still indispensable in the serious Christian life, it is even more strategic for churches to expect that every member be involved in a small group and a lay ministry, in outreach and mission. Most of all, lest their church be what C. S. Lewis called "a waste of time," they want their people "to draw men into Christ, to make them little Christs."

PERSPECTIVES ON RELEVANT CHRISTIANITY

There is no more explosive current issue in the churches of many lands, especially in the West, than the contest over "relevance." The term is not always used because the struggle usually fixates on more specific issues. The "church wars" about language, music, worship, and a range of style issues are symptoms of the underlying issue of relevance. The conflict goes deep and takes many forms. The issue is inescapable; no church is likely to get in step with early apostolic Christianity without finding a way through this thicket. The reflection in the next several pages will fully please no one and is likely to challenge everyone, because reality is more complex than the lens through which we have viewed it and the positions we have taken.[1]

Deep down, there is actually more agreement than churches usually experience. If by relevance we mean being meaningfully *connected*, almost all church leaders assume that Christianity *should* be relevant; the disagreements surface around questions like, Relevant to *what*, or to *whom*, or to *when*? For instance, some church leaders suppose that traditional European state-church Christianity is what Jesus and the apostles had in mind; so "our church" should connect with and duplicate the architecture, style, language, art, and music of the eighteenth-century German church whose people once crossed the ocean and established the tradition in North America. Other church leaders assume that the golden period to which we must stay connected is somewhat more recent—as in the churches devoted to keeping King James English and the music of Isaac Watts and Fanny Crosby alive. Other church leaders assume that the way they "do church" needs to remain connected to the current older members "who, after all, built this sanctuary and still pay the bills." Other church leaders are anxious to flex the church's approach to fit the church's young members, "lest we lose them." Still other church leaders want church to be relevant to seekers or to apathetic (or even antagonistic) pre-Christian people.[2]

If it is any comfort, leaders in many public sectors across the earth struggle with the relevance issue in some form. Theorists in fields like economics, political science, and environmental studies are expected to justify their existence by providing relevant intelligence for policy makers in government and other human affairs who have to understand and address complex changing conditions. Government leaders, in turn, are pressured to provide relevant policies and programs for the people. (Sam Rayburn, longtime Speaker of the U.S. House of Representatives, once confessed, "When I feel the heat, I see the light!") In all fields, the attainment of relevance seems to involve unlearning or sidelining old knowledge that has lived beyond the time of its relevance. If you once mastered Morse code or the slide rule or flannel graphing, for example, you no longer find much demand for that skill.

In the past quarter century, the distinct academic field of relevance theory has emerged.[3] One of the field's important insights addresses the traditional idea (since Aristotle) that communication is essentially the "transmission" of a message. In this traditional model, a communicator encodes a message for a receiver (who is assumed to possess an identical copy of the speaker's code system), who decodes it, and the message is thereby transmitted without serious loss or distortion. Relevance theorists believe that the transmission model has serious problems; most obvious, the receiver seldom possesses a sufficient copy of the communicator's code system, so effective communicators at least *adapt* to the receiver's code system.

Relevance theory, however, makes a very constructive contribution to our understanding of communication. The transmission of content is not the only thing going on when communication is effective. "Receivers" are not always mere passive receptors of messages. When communication is *really* effective, it is because the receiver is actively working to *infer* what the communicator *means*. Relevance theorists propose that an inferential model accounts for our most effective communication efforts better than a transmission model.

Relevance theory does not, of course, describe what actually happens in *most* communication efforts. Most receivers do *not* usually expend great mental effort to make sense of most of the messages that reach them; indeed, they often "tune out." Communicators, however, *can* activate the inferential process by adapting the message to stimulate the receiver's mind to seek understanding.

Relevance theorists seem to suggest that communicators do this in three ways (in, perhaps, ascending order of power): (1) by *adapting* to the audience's code system (mentioned previously); (2) by *connecting* their message to what the target receivers already assume, know, believe, or experience; and (3) by *engaging* the questions the target receivers are asking, the issues with which they struggle, and the needs and hopes that drive them.

Beyond what relevance theorists usually feature, I am convinced of another principle that accounts for the kind of communication that arouses the receiver's active desire to make sense of the message. People get actively involved with messages they find *interesting*. The most obvious example, within everyone's experience, is the power of narrative to trigger active inferring. The way people are engaged by, and become involved with, a detective story or a murder mystery, or good fiction or drama, may be explained more by narrative theory than by relevance theory—as usually represented.

In these three or four ways, then, receivers of messages *expect* the message to be relevant; if they perceive it as irrelevant, they have no reason to exert effort to understand it. Indeed, they often quit listening or reading. Most receivers need to perceive the message as relevant enough to expend the effort to process it.[4]

The late Lord Donald Soper, a British Methodist leader, reached a similar conclusion from his extensive experience in open-air advocacy: "We have to begin where people are, rather than where we would like them to be." I have reflected on Soper's insight for forty years. It is the seed of many strategic suggestions. For instance:

- We usually have to begin with pre-Christian people on *their turf*; most of them will never take the initiative to *engage* us inside our churches.

- We can usually begin with whatever people *already know* (that is sufficiently accurate) about Christianity and build on that.[5]

- We are called to communicate with pre-Christian people in *their language.* (They do not already possess the code systems of the church subculture or the theological academy.)

- We are called to *identify* with lost people who need to be found, and to *identify* with their issues, struggles, needs, hopes, and legitimate aspirations.[6]

- We are called to demonstrate the *relevance* of the message to their questions, issues, and legitimate aspirations. In the words of the Christmas hymn, we can demonstrate that "the hopes and fears of all the years are met in him tonight."

- We are called to show that the gospel is good news because it shows the way to the kind of self, the kind of life, and the kind of world that most people want.

It is difficult to doubt the power of ideas mediated through relevance. Scholars in the study of aesthetics, for instance, have recognized that if a painting or a music score is relevant to people's lives, it can change their perception of reality. Furthermore, we easily observe the impotence of art, music, and messages that people perceive as irrelevant.

◆   ◆   ◆   ◆

We encounter a different problem, however, when relevance is our *only* agenda, or when relevance (or anything else) becomes more important than *truth.* Relevance, after all, is *not* the *ultimate* value in effective communication. Artists know this. Even Thomas Kincaide, the "painter of light" who is often criticized for being "too popular," has declared, "The concept that an artist would be revered by popular culture is an immediate dismissal of his relevance as an artist."[7] In Christianity, we are the stewards of the revelation for all humankind. The target population is in no authoritative position to tell us what is true or not true, but only how to begin where they are in the biblical revelation's communication.

We find a version of the same problem (that perceived relevance is all that matters) in the widespread pragmatic approach to knowledge. Throughout most of my schooling, I sat close to someone who decided not to study some subject because, "In the real world, I will never need to know this." The first time I overheard something like this was in elementary school. We were learning the multiplication tables! This suggests, at least, that no one is able to predict with certainty what will be "useful" to know in the future. Christians, and even people in ordained ministry, are not immune from this barrier to education. I had colleagues in divinity school deciding whether to read a theology assignment on this criterion: "Will it preach?"

The problem is amplified when people are hijacked by anti-intellectualism. One day, on a website, I ran across a quotation by Thomas Fuller, a seventeenth-century

British writer, cleric, church historian, and friend of the rich and powerful: "'Tis not knowing much, but what is useful, that makes a wise man." While I am three or four centuries late, may I disagree? Knowing only "what is useful" does *not* make one "wise"; it does not even make one educated. After all, the first objective of education is to become educated, which happens from, and not without, some knowledge of the Bible, great literature, history, philosophy, math, science, geography, and cultures— whether we later "use" it all or not. A real education becomes the foundation from which a few people reach wisdom.

Of course, the Christian message, and Christianity itself, is enormously more than whatever some target population first perceives as relevant. Although we all have a pretty good sense of what we want, and hence what we think is relevant to our lives, none of us is the best judge of what, from God's perspective, we truly need. Effective Christianity *is* relevant to people's needs and issues, but it is never only that—any more than the vast continent, upon whose beach an exhausted swimmer first survives, is confined to that beach. (Tragically, *many* Christians misperceive Christianity as confined to what they originally understood and accepted. So, for some, Christianity is only about accepting Jesus as their savior so they can go to heaven one day and, until then, they attend church and live "a clean life.")

The problem surfaces from another direction when Christian spokespersons seem to *only* address the questions the target population is asking and the needs they feel. Christianity, to actually be *more* relevant, should also raise and address the questions that people *should* be asking but are not. So, for instance, if people are in denial about their addiction, or their mortality, or that justice and peace matter to God—whether they are interested yet or not—we are called to care enough to raise the question for them.

Christianity, however, is a greater continent than all of the possible answers to questions spoken and unspoken. Historically, in the catechism, we have immersed people in the Ten Commandments, the Lord's Prayer, and the Apostles' Creed— whether, at the moment, that material scratched where people itched or not. Moreover, we serve people best if we make it possible for them to root their consciousness in the Bible and Christian history, Augustine and the reformers, the saints and the martyrs, the theologians and the poets, Bach's B Minor Mass and Handel's *Messiah*, the Holy Land and the Sistine Chapel, Christian doctrine and Christian ethics, and more—whether every lesson in their Christian education delivers immediate gratification.

Nevertheless, most pre-Christian people have to experience Christianity as relevant or they never begin the adventure of following Christ. Second birth necessarily precedes much possibility of maturity. We have already delineated what it might be to "begin where people are" and why that is important. Three remaining topics—cultural relevance, emotional relevance, and a sublime expression of both—have the capacity to clarify and focus apostolic vision in thousands of places. The first two themes have experienced strange histories in the modern story of mission strategy; the third has usually been ignored. The first edged in from the side; the second was prominent in the first Great Awakening but has been neglected since; the third reaches us from the ancient Roman world, with several stops along the way.

40

The Stages of Mission and Cultural Relevance

One of Donald McGavran's most influential paradigms, his "Four Stages of Mission,"[8] has helped us understand that churches are *always* at some stage in mission, and it has helped churches locate the stage of mission in which history has placed them. I have, however, revised the paradigm to allow us to feature a supremely important factor in Christian mission that McGavran's stages model obscured.

I. A mission, in most any land and among most any group of people, begins at the *exploration* stage. McGavran cogently describes the typical tasks and experiences of the first pioneering overseas missionaries almost anywhere:

> This will mean finding a place to live, learning the language, being misunderstood, persecuted, banished, or killed, establishing beachheads of one sort or another, commending themselves by good works and holy lives, winning the first converts, and founding the first few congregations. Because the first congregations are started by outsiders, they will inevitably have a foreign flavor.[9]

McGavran explained that few of the nationals become Christians in this first stage because the barriers to following Christ are usually "more social than theological," and not enough nationals have become disciples for the people to perceive social permission to become Christians. The first converts may be perceived as leaving their community for the foreigners' community; some were already marginalized from their people.

II. McGavran identified the second stage as characterized by the establishment and ministries of *mission stations*. The mission builds a compound, usually enclosed, which provides missionary housing, a chapel, and facilities for other ministries, such as a literacy center or a school, a clinic or a hospital, a leprosy center or an agriculture training center. In time, the mission station employs some nationals. Mission station personnel typically work some beyond the compound. They may, for example, dig wells in nearby villages and plant several outpost congregations. But the mission supports the congregations financially and the congregations still have a foreign flavor. In any case, activities at the mission station still dominate whatever may happen in the hinterland and expatriates are still in charge, and they still do most of the ministry.

At this stage, no wider Christian movement is likely to occur and, unfortunately, *many* missions are arrested at this stage; indeed, they can become stuck at this stage for decades or even centuries. McGavran's most prophetic challenge to Christian mission came at this point. The mission station should always be a *temporary* stage in the mission's history. Strategic missions will move on to the third stage as soon as possible; indeed, one goal of the second stage should be to reach the third.

III. The third stage is the period of what I am calling *the national church*. Gifted citizens of the host nation are now in charge. Most of the pastors are nationals. Nationals now lead most of the ministries at the mission compound. Any missionaries who remain now fill in the gaps; they are now at the service of the national church's leaders.

This can be a difficult period as the first generation of national leaders learns to manage the institutions, programs, ministries, and congregations they inherited from the mission.[10] The sending church may still send some financial support; but long-term continued support may not be fully predictable.[11] But the national church is now largely *self-governing* and more *self-supporting* than it used to be, and *if* it can manage the transition to national leadership enough to focus outward, it often becomes much more *self-propagating* than when the missionaries were still in charge. The churches become less "foreign"; a college now prepares future pastors; the Bible and hymns are translated; many more churches are planted; and many churches grow, some contagiously. The life of the church and its people in the society now influences the wider public's perceptions of Christianity. McGavran explains:

> The good lives of Christians, the good deeds they do, their labors for justice and the public good, and the transformations of life that faith in Christ brings are noted by neighbors. The persecution and ostracism that plagued the early stages of the church die down. The church prospers and appears likely to survive. It becomes strong in more and more communities through the nation.[12]

At some point, the society gets used to some of its people becoming Christ-followers, and seekers experience more social clearance to explore the Way. When some particularly receptive clans, tribes, classes, or vocational groups turn more or less together to Christianity, the church becomes a Christian movement in some locales.

IV. The fourth stage involves the *substantial Christianization* of the society. Christianity is no longer a negligible minority movement in the land. In time, a critical mass of the population now confesses the Christian faith and "becoming a Christian" has now become a live option for their peers. Most nations, of course, are mosaics of many different peoples. By now, the national church is serving and planting churches in other demographic groups where the movement is positioned at an earlier stage of mission than in the population that is now substantially Christianized. In time, the younger church is now sending missionaries to other peoples within and beyond the borders of its nation-state. Some younger churches, such as the denominations of South Korea, are now sending out many more missionaries than they historically received.

McGavran observed that in stage four, evangelism now moves along three tracks. (1) The movement continues to reach more people in the population that is already substantially Christian. Indeed, they are more reachable now, and the movement has learned more about how to reach and disciple them. (2) The movement is now reaching across class, ethnic, and linguistic lines to reach peoples it had not reached before. (3) The movement is now, perhaps for the first time and especially in the cities, serving and evangelizing many kinds of people—"irrespective of homogeneous units."[13]

In the mission's fourth stage, the younger church is now typically producing four kinds of Christian communities.

- As it did from the mission's beginning, the movement continues to plant and grow "homogeneous unit" churches. Although anyone is welcome, the homogeneous unit church essentially serves one kind of people, such as people who share a common language or dialect, or a common background or condition (e.g., refugees or people who are blind).

- The denomination is also planting and growing "heterogeneous" churches, which reach and serve several kinds of people. McGavran observed that cities provide distinct opportunities for "conglomerate" churches.

- Many churches now proliferate congregations within the same church. It is not unusual for a church in Kuala Lumpur or many other cities to feature a dozen or more congregations within the same church. Some of the congregations are conglomerate; some are more homogeneous (for, say, Russian or Tagalog speakers, addicts, or people who are deaf); some offer contrasting liturgies—from classic and charismatic to jazz, rock, or healing services. Some of these churches also proliferate satellite campuses.

- The movement also produces specialized communities with causes. For instance, people from many churches, often from many cities and towns, whose Christian ethic has shaped a concern within them for justice or peace, literacy or education, for people who are blind or street children, for political reform or cross-cultural mission, will constitute a specific movement or organization devoted to advancing their cause.[14]

My refinement of McGavran's model comes at the third stage, which I have called the period of the national church, which McGavran called the "indigenous church" stage. McGavran drew from an earlier (now almost universally regarded as inadequate) understanding of what it means to be an indigenous church. Two nineteenth-century mission leaders, Melvin Hodges and Henry Venn, reasoned that when a younger church became "self-governing," "self-supporting," and "self-propagating," it was then, by definition, an indigenous church. McGavran did not always use the term "indigenous" in this dated nineteenth-century understanding, but in his stages model he did.

The "three-self" understanding that Hodges and Venn left us is now widely regarded as a necessary but not sufficient understanding of what makes a national church indigenous. For instance, most third-stage national churches are still scripted by Western theology, with theological conclusions that were once reached by challenges in (say) early medieval Europe that never were experienced by, for example, the people of China—an ancient and vast society with its own issues. As one example, China has a tradition of ancestor veneration, which has no significant counterpart in Europe's experience. Historically, when Chinese people have considered Christianity, they have inquired (for good reasons), "If we become Christians, what will we do with our ancestors?" The Western missionaries had no idea or they interpreted ancestor veneration as "idol worship" and seemed to require abandoning one's ancestors to become a Christian! Christianity has profound resources for reflecting on the issue, such as the affirmation in the Apostles' Creed that we believe in "the communion of saints." Our experience has demonstrated, however, that Chinese church leaders and theologians can more effectively reflect upon the meaning of such resources for their people than Western theologians can! So, from this and many other cases in mission's history, one can argue that another criterion for an indigenous church might be "self-theologizing."[15]

We can often observe other traits of the stage-three church that make movement to stage four difficult. Often, for instance, the national church leaders at stage three are more like the missionaries than they are like the nation's people. This should not surprise us. In many cases, the missionaries evangelized and discipled them; the missionaries were their role models; they worked side by side with the missionaries; and, in many fields, the missionaries groomed them to be the first generation of national leaders. Often, the designated national leaders earn a degree in Europe or North America at the very institution where the missionaries studied. The people typically are glad that citizens of their nation are in charge, but they comment that their bishop "is not really one of us."

At this national (but not yet indigenous) stage, the people still experience some things as culturally alien about their national church. The hymns are now translated into their tongue, but they are still Western hymns, perhaps played on an organ. Their chapel's architecture may be more like chapels in England or New England than like other buildings in the community. The first full translation of the Bible is almost always a wooden translation—a heroic first draft but not yet a literature that fits the people.

We could list more examples, but the point is now almost obvious. A national church, with some of the nation's citizens in charge, is not yet an indigenous church until the church is indigenous in the sense of *cultural relevance*. When the church is indigenous in this sense, when not only the indigenous language but all of the culture's *forms* are used to communicate and celebrate the gospel's *meaning*, then the Christian faith has a fair chance to become contagious in the society. Adapting to the host culture's style, language, music, aesthetics, architecture, and so on, is apostolic Christianity's way to identify with the people and extend the Incarnation.

So we are now clearer than our predecessors were that each people's *culture* is the natural medium of God's supernatural revelation to them. When the gospel treasure is expressed in alien cultural forms, they may not "get it" or understand that the message was sent with them in mind. We are also clearer than before that the gospel is especially transformative if its indigenous expression engages the *worldview* of the people. ("Worldview" refers to the small constellation of beliefs and values that are so central in the culture that, together, they provide the "lens" through which the people perceive the world, life, and reality.)[16]

So a Christian mission is planted, develops, and becomes reproductive in five stages:

1. The Exploration Stage

2. The Mission Station Stage

3. The National Church Stage

4. The Indigenous Church Stage

5. The Substantial Christianization Stage

I have summarized some of the indispensable insights from cultural anthropology and about indigenous Christianity in other writings.[17] While I stand by those writings, I have learned that monocultural readers need to read more than a chapter. The literature of missionary anthropology teaches these insights with more thoroughness than we can in Church Growth books.[18]

Readers experience their most important single discovery when they learn to distinguish between *form* and *meaning*. (Like everything else, this is more complex than it should be.) Essentially, however, the communication of meaning takes place *through* language and also through a range of other symbols and symbolic expressions such as gesture, tone, and facial expression, as well as music, dance, architecture, and other aesthetic expressions. Any serious symbolic expression, such as "God loves you," has limited power to communicate what is fully meant. But we can express it many times, in many ways, through several senses; and the receiver thinks about it, the receiver group talks about it, and in time the group *may* experience an understanding or perspective similar to what the communicator had in mind. Two-way conversation *between* the communicator and receiver can overcome much misunderstanding and reduce the gap.

Anyone who has ever been married or raised children can testify that communication is a complex process. We are often mysteries to one another and sometimes to ourselves. The challenge becomes more formidable when we are attempting to inform or influence someone we have not known who is beyond our family, social unit, generation, or subculture. Once, as a doctoral student in communication studies, I discovered that the communication of the meaning of Christianity's message to people with no Christian memory or background is so complex that, humanly speaking, it ought never happen! (If Paul had not already informed us, "No one can say 'Jesus is Lord' except by the Holy Spirit," I *might* have figured that out!) *If* there are language or cultural barriers between communicator and audience, the chances of meaning "leaking" through our communication efforts is reduced even more.

This is why, in working to "indigenize" Christianity's expression, we need to *adapt* to the style, language, aesthetics, and music of the target population. Gospel communication across cultures, or subcultures, or even between generations, involves unwrapping the gospel from the cultural "clothing" in which we received it and rewrapping it in the target population's clothing. If we pay the price to reach them through their language and other cultural forms, this does not guarantee that they will become Christ-followers; but we have removed the culture barrier, so the gospel now has a fair chance among them. Informed missionaries *can* often communicate effectively enough to reach perhaps ten or twenty of the most receptive people; then, as the converts communicate naturally with their peers, a Christian movement becomes possible.

Recovering the Emotional Relevance of "a Religion of the Heart"

In a presentation to an annual gathering of "tall steeple" Presbyterian pastors, I presented "A Case for Culturally Relevant Christianity." Indigenous Christianity, I suggested, is as indispensable for reaching pre-Christian people in the United States as in any other mission field on earth. The other presenter was Archibald Hart, dean emeritus of Fuller's School of Psychology. After affirming my case, he asked a penetrating question: "Who is making the case for *emotionally* relevant Christianity?" I sensed, instantly, that he was right. Indeed, I had studied the rationale for "emotional appeals" in rhetorical theory for years but had insufficiently connected those studies to my broader interests in how the gospel engages pre-Christian people.

The case for emotional relevance is more easily made than for cultural relevance. The emotional lives of a great many pre-Christian people (and some Christian people) are dysfunctional, out of control, and crippling their lives. We meet individuals and families every day whose lives are hijacked by powerful emotions they do not understand and may even deny. David Seamands exposed the fact that many people exist with "damaged emotions," especially guilt, depression, low self-esteem, and perfectionism, which need healing.[19]

Furthermore, Christian salvation essentially involves "being made whole," which includes deliverance from emotions that were destroying our souls and deliverance into the life of the kingdom of God in which we experience a new emotional world. I have interviewed many converts who report such a change; the old feelings may still visit, but they no longer have dominion. Christian experience has essentially liberated them from the narcissism, the unmanaged anger, the low self-esteem, the envy, and the pervasive anxiety that were undermining their happiness; and Christian experience has freed them to experience gratitude, hope, empathy, altruism, and appropriate self-love, and to become (as promised in Reinhold Niebuhr's "Serenity Prayer") "reasonably happy in this life," as a foretaste of being "supremely happy with Him forever in the next."

Crash Course in Human Emotion Theory

Scholars have struggled to make sense of human emotional experience ever since Aristotle first reflected on "the passions," though the quest became somewhat more scientific with the reflections of William James and Sigmund Freud. In twenty-five centuries, the quest has not reached anything approaching a unanimous understanding, though the following insights may represent a near consensus.

We are both rational and emotional creatures, though we have usually emphasized the rational. As in Descartes's "I think, therefore I am," the ideology of the European Enlightenment defined human beings essentially as rational beings. Although we still experience emotions, they represent a "lower" part of human nature from which evolution has only partly delivered us. Nevertheless, human reason can and should trump emotion, and education's mission is to perfect humans for a life of reason. In time, the Enlightenment separated Western humanity from nature and produced the culture of modernity and a more scientific, planned, mechanized modern world in which, especially in cities, many people experienced estrangement from nature, alienation from others, and a depersonalization of the self.

Whereas the Enlightenment promoted the way of reason, logic, and science in all matters, the romanticism of the eighteenth and nineteenth centuries challenged modernity's full-court press. In literature, drama, music, and the visual arts, the Romantics rediscovered "the heart" and the roles of intuition, imagination, passion, mystery, and the supernatural, as well as the mystical, harmony with nature, and faith.

William Wordsworth invited readers to disengage from the arid worldview of science and reengage nature, "and bring with you a heart / That watches and receives." William Blake invited us to "see a World in a Grain of Sand And a Heaven in a Wild Flower."

The quest to understand emotionality within human nature has become more nuanced in the last century. We can almost summarize the state of our basic "emotional intelligence" in the following baker's dozen statements:[20]

1. We can define an emotion as a rather specific internal affective state; a mood, by comparison, is a less specific and more background internal affective state.

2. Many scholars conclude that there are a limited number of basic emotions that all or most people experience, such as happiness, anger, sadness, and fear. (Some pop psychologists refer to them as "glad, mad, sad, and anxious"!) Some scholars add disgust, shame, and guilt to their list of basic emotions.

3. We are thought to have "families" of related emotions, and family members may vary from one another, in part, in their intensity. So sadness is related to grief, happiness is related to ecstasy, and anger is related to rage; in each pairing, the latter is more intense.

4. Some emotions may be blends of basic emotions. So rage is thought to be a blend of anger and fear; and jealousy a blend of fear, anger, and sadness.

5. An emotion may not be stable; so love, for instance, can morph into jealousy or grief.

6. Emotions typically vary in their duration. So the experience of being surprised may be brief; fear may last much longer; and the experience of anxiety or vengeance may stretch over years or a lifetime.

7. Many scholars have been clear, since the publication of Aristotle's *Art of Rhetoric*, that these internal affective states are responses to objects or events in the external world. So, for instance, anger is often a response to a perceived slight, offense, or wrong. An emotion, therefore, is a way in which we respond to the world or engage with the world.

8. Emotion is not different from reason in the sense that you can put them at opposite ends of a spectrum. Human emotion contains its own kind of intelligence. We often reach insights intuitively that we could not have reached through reasoning. Emotion, however, is not always intelligent. Love can be fooled; fear can slide into phobia.

9. We now know what once we would have never guessed: that our powers of reason are dependent upon our emotions to function effectively. At one level, we have known that anxiety, fear, or anger makes our best thinking unavailable to us; but we now know that effective reasoning is *dependent* upon emotions conducive to thinking. Antonio Demasio studied people who had brain damage in the brain's emotional centers. He discovered that the loss of the capacity to feel distorts a person's decision making. Emotionally impaired people can still do math or understand a puzzle, but without the relevant emotional support they do not make rational decisions—like where to invest their savings—because they do not care.[21]

10. Our emotions do not "just happen to us," nor are they usually an automatic response to a stimulus. The field of symbolic interactionism, pioneered by George Herbert Mead, has helped us see that our own internal conversation often "constructs" the emotion with which we respond to a situation. Essentially, when something

47

happens, our *internal conversation* stimulates an emotional state in which our continuing internal conversation (now influenced by what we are feeling) governs the action we will take. The process can be graphed:

Event————Self-talk————Feelings————More Self-talk————Action

11. We are now clearer than before that we can have more control over our emotions than we once thought—largely by controlling our internal conversation. So students have learned to "psych" themselves up for an exam, and the sports psychologists who teach and counsel athletes to prepare for peak performance are becoming as indispensable to championships as strength coaches.

12. Some emotions, such as fear and maybe anger, may be physiologically hardwired within us, though we interpret an emotional experience through our language, and our culture shapes how we express our emotions. (Arabs, for instance, typically express anger very differently from Chinese people.) Most of our other emotions are shaped more by our enculturation and life experience than by physiology.

13. The terms *emotions* and *feelings* are not synonymous. Emotions are more primary and run deeper; feelings are related to the physiological symptoms (as in increased heart rate or sweaty palms) of our emotions.

Many rhetorical theorists since Aristotle have almost assumed that human beings are essentially *emotional* creatures who are sometimes capable of thinking! Or at the least, any public communicator must take human emotions seriously and include appropriate "emotional appeals" in speaking or writing. A speech's introduction needs to be emotionally engaging enough to secure the attention of many auditors; and the speech's conclusion must elicit enough emotional response for many auditors to act on what they now believe. As Reinhold Niebuhr once reported from pastoral experience, in *Leaves from the Notebook of a Tamed Cynic*, many or most people will not act in response to a proposal if they are merely convinced that the message is true and that acting on it is their "duty"; they must be sufficiently "moved" to act. George Campbell, in *The Philosophy of Rhetoric*, declared, "To say that it is possible to persuade without speaking to the passions is but, at best, a kind of specious nonsense.... Passion is the mover to action, reason is the guide."[22]

Understanding human emotions is not important to us only because their dysfunctional forms can be so destructive. Understanding emotions helps us empathize with one another and live in community. Understanding emotions helps us enjoy animals, who lack our intelligence but share much of our emotional repertoire. A healthy emotional life fills our lives with much meaning and satisfaction. How we manage, and act upon, our emotions repeatedly and habitually over time substantially shapes our character and the kind of person we become.

Protestant Christianity's Pioneer in Emotionally Relevant Ministry

Jonathan Edwards (1703–58), leader of America's first Great Awakening and arguably America's greatest theologian and philosopher, also pioneered as a de facto

Church Growth scholar. As the reflective leader of an "awakening," he employed field observation, interviews, and historical analysis (in addition to biblical and theological reflection) to make sense of a Christian movement, to lead and advance his movement and others, and also to make sense of a movement's subsequent decline and the loss of many of its converts, who had reverted to the world.

In the 1730s, Edwards was pastor of the church in Northampton, Massachusetts. Edwards tells us that the town had approximately two hundred families (a large town in the colonial era). The church also served people who lived in several outlying hamlets. An awakening broke out among some young people in 1733, and spread to others in 1734 and 1735. Edwards observed, "More than 300 souls were savingly brought home to Christ in this town in the space of half a year."[23] In one five- or six-week period, about thirty people per week became Christians.

Edwards *studied* this movement that God entrusted to him; he wrote case studies of a number of converts and he discerned, with remarkable sophistication, a number of patterns that helped account for the awakening. He presented his firsthand report, analyses, insights, and conclusions in his *Faithful Narrative of the Surprising Work of God* (1737). The book rapidly became the text for expanding the awakening across much of colonial America and, through translations, across much of Europe as well.

For instance, Edwards rooted his analysis in the community's history and demographics. Compared to many communities, Northampton's people were fairly sober, orderly, reasonable, and less prone to vice—"a good sort of people." Edwards noticed that the people "dwell more compactly together"[24] than in most towns; so when several people experienced conversion, their proximity to their neighbors contributed to the movement's contagion. The church in Northampton had a history of sound doctrine and freedom from serious divisions, and had already experienced several "ingatherings" in its history; so the church and people knew what was possible and perhaps expected God to act again. In the period right before the awakening, however, the town deteriorated into hostile factionalism and increased immorality; then they experienced a period of greater religious seriousness and receptivity.

The awakening actually broke out in Pascommuck, a village three miles from Northampton. Following the deaths of a teenage boy and a young married woman, "there began evidently to appear more of a religious concern on people's minds."[25] Edwards gathered Pascommuck's young people for teaching, after which they met in lay-led small groups for "social religion." The youth groups continued meeting and adult groups also formed. "There were, very suddenly, one after another, five or six persons who were to all appearance savingly converted."[26] These converts profoundly influenced others, and Pascommuck Christians reported what God was doing to the Northampton church.

These reports apparently catalyzed the awakening in Northampton, and Edwards similarly deployed laity to testify from town to town throughout the awakening's expansion. He continued to organize people into many lay-led small "religious societies" throughout the awakening. During each week, Edwards intentionally engaged people, one-on-one, in "private conference"; he seems to have listened more than he talked. He noticed that converts, and even excited visitors, conversed with friends and neighbors about what was happening, and he encouraged the ministry of conversation with seekers.

Edwards's preaching style changed. He began preaching in a much more vivid imaginative style, which engaged people more emotionally than in traditional Puritan discourse. His most anthologized sermon, "Sinners in the Hands of an Angry God," was probably his most extreme experiment in imaginal preaching.

Edwards observed then that Northampton's congregation reflected a heightened expectation.

> Our public assemblies were then beautiful; the congregation was alive in God's ser-
> vice, everyone earnestly intent on public worship, every hearer eager to drink in the
> words of the minister as they came from his mouth; the assembly in general were, from
> time to time, in tears while the Word was preached; some weeping with sorrow and
> distress, others with joy and love, others with pity and concern for the souls of their
> neighbors.[27]

Much of the rest of Edwards's *Faithful Narrative* reports the emotional experiences of the people—prior to conversion and after.

Edwards observed that in the period before conversion, people typically experience a period of spiritual and emotional struggle. They may be "seized with convictions" about their pride or unbelief, or disturbed in their conscience. They may feel shame, fear, misery, unworthiness, "distresses of thought," or even depression. They may envy Christians—especially new Christians. Edwards perceived, "The awful apprehensions persons have had of their misery, have for the most part been *increasing*, the nearer they have approached to deliverance."[28] Often, they "never think of themselves so far off from as when they are nearest."[29] He perceived that people who are awakened but not yet converted often begin responding in two ways: (1) They abandon some of their "sinful practices, . . . vices, and extravagancies," and they (2) become actively involved with "the means of salvation—reading, prayer, meditation, the ordinances of God's house, and private conference."[30] As they get closer to conversion, often "their affections are moved, and they are full of tears, in their confessions and prayers."[31]

Edwards discovered that conversion (as saving grace discovered and experienced), involved profound changes in the people's emotional lives. Although the emotional range varied from one personality to another, new Christians typically experienced a calmness of spirit and a new love for God, people, and creation, as well as peace, compassion, empathy, hope, and especially "joy in Christ." "Their hearts are often touched, and sometimes filled, with new sweetnesses and delights; there seems to be an inward burning of heart that they express, the like to which they never experienced before."[32]

In another significant insight, Edwards observed that because seekers in distress often did not realize how close to the kingdom they were, likewise, "before their own conversions they had very imperfect ideas of what conversion was."[33] (One person's conversion experience scripted the neighbors' expectations of what they would experience, but the latter's experience was often so different that they wondered whether they were yet Christians. When Edwards perceived "the fruits of the Spirit" in their life, *he* would assure them, verbally, that they now belonged to Christ.) So, "the surprising work of God" surprised the converts as much as it surprised Edwards!

In the two-year awakening in Northampton and the surrounding county, Edwards observed the movement reaching all sorts of people. Unlike Northampton's earlier ingatherings, this one reached as many males as females, and it reached people across the age span. The local awakening reached "sober and vicious, high and low, rich and poor, wise and unwise; it reached the most considerable families and persons, to all appearances, as much as others."[34]

Late in the Northampton awakening, Edwards observed that religious *emotionalism* could be counterproductive; when two religious men acted out on "strange enthusiastic delusions," the "instances of conversion" became "rare."[35]

◆　　◆　　◆　　◆

Edwards concluded his *Faithful Narrative* with, overall, an optimistic appraisal of the awakening. Although a few apparent converts had relapsed, most of the people "thought to be converted among us . . . generally seem to be persons that have had an abiding change wrought on them."[36] In later years, however, many of those people reverted back to the world and to their former way of life.

Jonathan Edwards's observation of this undeniable fact, followed by additional field research and reflection, led to some of the most important strategic reflections in the history of evangelical Christianity. He now asked how one distinguished between valid Christian experience and its unstable counterfeit. In his *Faithful Narrative* he had identified those converts who then appeared to be enduring Christians with traits like "new views of God" and a sense of "the great things of the gospel," and with "hearts" that had been "touched."[37] When he later observed that a number of *those* converts had lapsed, his research and reflection produced an astonishing range of deeper insights, which were published in 1746 in his *Treatise Concerning Religious Affections*.

Part one of *Religious Affections* is a measured defense of the role of emotions within Christian experience. Edwards reflects a knowledge of human emotions that is remarkably congruent with today's lore. Our "passions" or "affections" are not automatic responses, nor do they happen to us; they are "the more vigorous and sensible exercises of the inclination and will of the soul."[38] Furthermore, the heart's affections are "the spring of men's actions."[39] Human nature is "very inactive" unless "influenced by some affection, either love or hatred, desire, hope, fear or some other. These affections we see to be the springs that set men agoing, in all the affairs of life, and engage them in all their pursuits."[40]

Edwards now observed that emotional religious experiences can be excessive, and a religious experience is no guarantee that the person will be a Christian for life. He reflected that colonial Christian history had shifted between extremes. In one period, we "look[ed] upon all high religious affections" as evidence of "true grace," and we accepted all "religious talk" as a sign of the Spirit. More recently, "instead of esteeming and admiring all religious affections, without distinction, it is . . . more prevalent to reject and to discard all without distinction."[41]

Nevertheless, he contended, "True religion, in great part, consists in the affections."[42] Christianity without passion is powerless and lifeless. Indeed, emotional religious experience is essential in both the conversion and in the later renewal of souls.

> That religion which God requires, and will accept, does not consist in weak, dull, and lifeless wouldings, raising us but a little above a state of indifference;...A fervent, vigorous engagedness of the heart...is the fruit of a real circumcision of the heart, or true regeneration, and that has the promises of life.... Nor was there ever a saint awakened out of a cold lifeless frame, or recovered from a declining state in religion, and brought back from a lamentable departure from God, without having his heart affected.[43]

So Edwards's purpose in the *Treatise Concerning Religious Affections* is to "distinguish between affections."[44]

Part two of *Religious Affections*, after two and half centuries, *still* serves as a challenge to the assumptions that prevail in most churches today. He identifies a dozen "signs" that are widely assumed to be signs of grace, conversion, and the Spirit, but they are *not necessarily* so. Essentially, Edwards discovered the following:

- If people have had great emotional religious experiences, they may or may not be Christians who will endure.

- If people can quote many texts of Scripture, they may or may not be Christians years from now.

- If people are "fluent, fervent and abundant in talking of the things of religion,"[45] they may be the kind of Christians God wants, but not necessarily.

- If people can give moving testimonies, they may or may not be the real thing.

- If people attend church and they perform other religious duties with zeal, they may or may not be New Testament Christians.

Edwards says more, but this is enough to follow his still revolutionary insight. He learned from his involvement in the awakening that such signs as emotional religious experiences, learning Scripture, talking the faith, and so on are essential to authentic enduring conversion, but you cannot tell by *those* traits who will likely be Christians for the long haul and who will not.

In part three of *Religious Affections*, Jonathan Edwards unpacked what he *now* understood to be among the "distinguishing signs of truly gracious and holy affections." Edwards gives us another dozen more valid signs of the Christianity that lasts, offering them more for self-examination than for appraising others. He suggested that the following three are the most normative:

1. People who have experienced "a change of nature,"[46] which family and friends, the church, and lost people can clearly perceive, will likely endure. Christian experience, Edwards reminds us, is supposed to be "transforming." Grace changes people with respect to their "natural temperament"; although the temperament may not be completely "rooted out," there is evidence of a

"great alteration." Grace changes people with respect to "whatever is sinful" in them; although they may still experience temptation, their former sins "no longer have dominion" over them. "Therefore if there be no great and remarkable abiding change in persons that think they have experienced a work of conversion, vain are all their imaginations and pretenses, however they have been affected."[47]

2. Edwards declared, "Christian practice" is "the chief of all the signs of grace."[48] Valid Christians follow Jesus and live by his ethic. What people *do* and how they *live* is the surest sign of the state of their hearts. Essentially, this means that they live in compassionate goodwill toward people and other creatures; that they live by "the will of God" and no longer for their own selfish agenda; that, consistent with their gifts from the Spirit, they are involved in ministry in the church and beyond; and that their lives will "bear fruit."[49] The point in becoming a Christian, after all, is *not* simply to go to heaven and experience Christ's other benefits, but to become agents of God's new creation.

3. Edwards stressed that people who are changed and obeying God's will do not become this way and live this way by their own power or effort alone. They need more grace and Holy Spirit within them than they first experienced when they became new disciples, and this additional grace comes to those who deeply accept Jesus Christ as Lord (and not as Savior only) and who are really open to his Spirit. The source of the life that we want to live is supernatural. IF we will let God get as close to us as God wants to, we will see the world more like God does, and we will live by God's power a life we could not live by a lifetime of New Year's resolutions.[50]

Emotional Relevance in Ministry Today

Today most church leaders function as though the emotional part of human nature does not need to be taken seriously (or they take it seriously in counseling only). Their leaders observe that emotions sometimes get in the way in congregational life or become dysfunctional in persons and families, but these are "aberrations" and what people really need is sound doctrine and religious advice. Jonathan Edwards's discoveries that "true religion, in great part, consists in the affections" and that people need to be liberated from the power of emotions such as fear and misery and need to experience emotions like peace and joy have been substantially lost, even in Edwards's reformed tradition.

There are exceptions. Some pastors who are schooled in the advanced art of pastoral counseling have developed other ways to be emotionally relevant in the church's life. Some churches that launch recovery ministries for people with addictions learn to help with the fear, resentment, guilt, shame, low self-esteem, and the extreme mood swings that typically afflict addicts and, from that ministry, they learn to engage other people's emotional needs as well.

In contrast to the mainline churches whose paradigm of human nature is still rooted in the Enlightenment, most of the Christian movements today have found pathways to people's emotional worlds. The Inuit Christian movement began, in many Arctic communities, with people who had addictions, and the movement has learned to engage their people's feelings in conversations, small groups, prayer meetings, and even in cathartic experiences in public worship. Tim Keller, who has led Redeemer Presbyterian Church's growth in Manhattan, is deeply rooted in Jonathan Edwards's *Treatise Concerning Religious Affections*, which, he reports, has provided an "indispensable foundation" for accessing more current perspectives on human emotion.

In a conversation with Archibald Hart, we brainstormed some of the basic ways that churches can, and sometimes do, become emotionally relevant. A church's leaders might begin by paying closer attention to the emotional life of the people. For instance, about one in seven or eight people experiences depression; addiction to multiple substances and processes is very widespread; and many people are stuck in "learned hopelessness." Effective churches will have learned to name, identify with, and connect with people's emotional needs; often, church leaders help people get over the denial in their emotional lives. Making human emotions a prominent and continuing topic in the church's life works wonders over time.

Emotionally relevant ministries will provide people with help, support, insight, options, and especially perspective. People need insight on how much stress assaults their lives, and perspective on how "living outside of God's design" magnifies the stress. They need to know that the gospel is good news for their struggle and that the Holy Spirit paces the floor with them. Effective churches will take a very redundant approach to emotional engagement through many lay-led addiction recovery groups, divorce recovery groups, and other support groups; through ministries of intercession; and through the liturgical ministry of the church—from the sermon to the music to the ministry of testimony to the pastoral prayer. Testimonies help people discover they are not alone in struggling with, for example, a phobia. The pastoral prayer will be honest and specific, and will thereby *model* how people can pray about their emotional pain. "Most people haven't a clue," Hart reflected.

I asked Hart, "What churches are practicing what you preach?" He mentioned one church—Saddleback Valley Community Church in Orange County, California. Rick Warren, Saddleback's founding pastor, planted the church in 1979 with a founding vision to be "a place where the hurting, depressed, frustrated, and confused can find help." Warren studied with Hart in Saddleback's early years, and he has steered Saddleback in emotionally relevant directions ever since. In Saddleback's early years, Warren's preaching often targeted people who felt they were "falling apart" or that their lives were "out of control." His series on the seven deadly sins was emotionally focused. (The sermon on greed, for instance, asked, "Why do I always feel like I have to have more? No matter how much I get, I have to have more! Why do I have that feeling?") In recent years, Warren has often featured sermons or sermon series focused explicitly on topics like pressure, depression, anger, self-esteem, and burnout. Saddleback's services feature a testimony, often reporting the person's emotional deliverance by grace. Much of Saddleback's worship music, from the singing ensemble's performance on stage to the congregation's singing, heads straight for the heart—engaging emotional issues, celebrating a gospel of deliverance, and radiating hope, accompanied and sung with unrestrained passion. Rick Warren's book *The Purpose Driven Life* has sold more than twenty-five million copies, in part because it addresses some of people's emotional struggles so clearly.

In 1991, Saddleback's John Baker built upon the twelve steps of Alcoholics Anonymous to pioneer "Celebrate Recovery," a ministry for people with addictions. In time, they perceived that many people who do not have substance addictions nevertheless struggle with obsessions or other problems in which the same emotional issues are at the core, and the same twelve steps bring them restoration and recovery. Celebrate Recovery is now designed to help anyone "overcome their hurts, habits, and hang-ups." The Friday evening ministry (which includes a meal, a large group worship with a lecture or testimony, then small group meetings for people with similar "hurts, hang-ups, and habits," and ends with the Solid Rock Café social time) has served more than 8,000 people at Saddleback's campus. When they started the ministry, 70 percent of attendees were from the church and 30 percent were from the community; today 70 percent are from the community. The church has expanded Celebrate Recovery's reach to junior high and senior high students. Hundreds of other churches and a number of prisons have adapted Celebrate Recovery to their context.

More broadly, Saddleback ministers with whole persons, including their emotions, through more than 1,400 lay-led small groups. Partly because some of our emotional needs (such as for purpose or significance) are only met as a by-product of being in ministry with others, Saddleback features a seminar for "turning an audience into an army." People discover their spiritual gifts, heart, abilities, personality type, and significant experiences, and thereby discover how God has "SHAPEd" them for a specific ministry. Thousands of Saddleback's people are involved in a ministry based on their SHAPE. Saddleback now sponsors more than 300 community ministries, engaging such target groups as prisoners, CEOs, addicts, single parents, people who are homeless, and people with HIV/AIDS. Saddleback believes that *all* people can inhabit a new emotional world of the Spirit and know hope, inner strength, peace, joy, and a life of purpose, passion, and adventure.

On Recovering Sublime Experience in Communicating Christianity

Occasionally, communication experience engages people more deeply, pervasively, profoundly, and with more emotional power than most scholars even pretend to account for.[51] In the last 2,000 years, however, one theory, the theory of the sublime, has surfaced from time to time to substantially account for the most profound and transformative kind of communication experience. The theory explains why unusual power is sometimes experienced when imagination, indigenous aesthetic expression, and emotional engagement come together in the same event.

A first-century Roman rhetorical theorist, whom the tradition knows as Longinus, emphasized the role of transcendent emotion in oral and written discourse. He was interested in the emotive power of language, and he perceived that "sublime" expression (oral, written, or dramatized) amplifies the emotional experience of discourse. Sometimes, he observed, public discourse can so enthrall audiences and readers that it transports people into such a transcendent emotional state of consciousness that they become convinced on nonrational (though not necessarily irrational) grounds that the truth claim or rhetorical vision *must* be true. Something like the awe that we can experience in observing a natural wonder can also be experienced through an encounter with magnificent music (like Bach's Mass in B Minor) or great art and architecture (like Michelangelo's Sistine Chapel) or a great speech (like Martin Luther King Jr.'s "I Have a Dream" speech).

Our occasional experiences can confirm Longinus's big idea. We have all been so powerfully engaged by some aesthetic experiences—perhaps from a great moment in film, poetry, or music—that we were inclined to believe whatever message it served! As Aristotle reminded us, however, the three modes of persuasion (*logos, ethos,* and *pathos*), quite including the use of emotional power in the arts and public address, can be used for good or for evil. For example, the Russian people sometimes experienced sublime power in Lenin's speeches, and the Third Reich used the emotionally compelling music of Wagner to engage and stir the masses. Aristotle argued, however, that the possible misuse of knowledge about communication effectiveness is NO reason to abandon such knowledge. Truth, he said, is more powerful than its opposite, but it needs advocates who are schooled in the communication arts to represent truth to audiences; the con men, marketing gurus, charlatans, and demagogues learn all they can about engaging audiences. Advocates who know the truth, he warned, must not abandon truth naked before its enemies.

We have inherited only most of Longinus's *On the Sublime* (some fragments were lost over time), but the text we have is enormously significant. The word *sublime* is rooted in the Latin *sublimes*, which suggested looking up, or being raised to great height. Longinus observed:

> Sublimity,... produced at the right moment, tears everything up like a whirlwind, and exhibits the orator's whole power at a single blow.... Real sublimity contains much food for reflection, is difficult or rather impossible to resist and makes a strong and ineffaceable impression on the memory.... Sublimity is always an eminence and excellence in language; and that from this, and this alone, the greatest poets and writers of prose have attained the first place and have clothed their fame in immortality. For it is not to persuasion but to **ecstasy** that passages of extraordinary genius carry the hearer.[52]

More than the other classical rhetoricians, Longinus stressed the power of the imaginative communication of great thought to "elevate," to "uplift," and to "transport" people out of themselves and so to see their world differently.

Sublime discourse, Longinus observed, can engage a remarkable range of human beings in the same interacting audience, which amplifies people's sense that the message *must* be true. The shared experience of being a member of an enthralled audience produces shared meanings and convictions, and a shared identity, in a previously heterogeneous audience. Longinus clarified the "five most productive sources of sublimity" in oral and written discourse:

1. Great ideas

2. Strong and inspired emotion

3. Certain figures of speech

4. An elevated and noble tone of expression

5. Dignified and elevated word arrangement

In time, Longinus's treatise was all but forgotten until its translation into French in the sixteenth century. In the last four centuries, however, a number of thinkers and movements have stood on Longinus's shoulders. His theory now helps explain the most powerful (though occasional) kind of experience in public life. A range of writers and schools of thought has reflected on sublime theory in recent centuries. The following may be especially instructive for evangelization.

Edmund Burke (1729–97, Irish philosopher and statesman in Great Britain's House of Commons), in A *Philosophical Enquiry into the Origin of Our Ideas on the Sublime and the Beautiful,* suggested that populations who struggle; who experience difficulty, pain, danger, or terror; or who are concerned for their lives, may be especially open to or needing sublime experiences that lift them up. Burke believed that the capacity for sublime experience is rooted in human physiology and psychology. He contrasted our experiences of beauty and sublimity: beauty engages the serene, harmonious *feminine* part of human nature; sublimity engages the rougher, more turbulent *masculine* dimension within us. (Sublime experience is, therefore, a promising way to reach men.) Sublime experience catalyzes the capacity within us to think differently about a matter than we did before; sometimes the sublime experience "anticipates our reasonings, and hurries us on by an irresistible force."

Immanuel Kant (1724–1804, philosopher in the late Enlightenment period and influenced by Burke), boldly included aesthetics within philosophy's scope. He reflected on the mystery of sublime experience in *Observations on the Feeling of the Beautiful and Sublime* (1784) and in the chapter "Analytic of the Beautiful" in his later *Critique of Judgment.* He wrote, "We call that sublime which [we experience as] absolutely great." Sublime experience involves human understanding and imagination, but it is much more a subjective aesthetic experience than an objective logical conclusion. The experience is a deep subjective response to something perceived as so "absolutely great" that it cannot be quantified or measured; the experience is one of deep delight, from which people may respond in deeper thought or commitment.

Many writers and thinkers of and following the Romantic period reacted against the Age of Reason, and they substantially reemphasized the role of powerful emotions in human experience—including sublime experience (though not always employing the term). **Victor Hugo** called for authors and artists to make sublime experience possible for people, and people experienced many of his poems as sublime. Writers on both sides of the Atlantic, including William Blake, William Wordsworth, Samuel Taylor Coleridge, Robert Browning and Elizabeth Barrett Browning, and Thomas De Quincey in Great Britain; and Vachel Lindsay, Henry Wadsworth Longfellow, James

Russell Lowell, John Greenleaf Whittier, and Ralph Waldo Emerson in the United States, often appealed directly and deeply to the hearts of readers. Matthew Arnold's literary theory established a place for the sublime doctrine in the British academy. The Romantics helped pave the way for "the religion of the heart," championed by Jonathan Edwards and John Wesley, which catalyzed the Great Awakening in North America and western Europe. In time, however, the theory's currency was devalued; anything that merely inspired someone was now regarded as "sublime"!

Søren Kierkegaard (1813–55), in works like *Attack Upon Christendom*, *Edifying Discourses*, *Either/Or*, and *Fear and Trembling*, reflected upon the Christendom period of his native Denmark, which was now a spent force. "When everybody is a 'Christian'" (as citizens of a so-called Christian country), he contended, "nobody is a Christian" (in the New Testament sense of a follower of Christ). Kierkegaard contended that it may be futile to attempt the direct communication of Christianity's message to people who had heard it so many times before that they assumed they already understood it and were immunized against its full power. So he advocated an indirect approach to communicating Christian truth, in which the preacher or writer, through narrative and imaginative expression, helps the receiver "discover" Christian truth claims as for the first time and with the experiential power that overcomes the immunization.

Although **Rudolph Otto**'s *Idea of the Holy* (1869–1937) does not cite Kierkegaard's work, Otto continued Kierkegaard's move to ground the theory theologically more than before, and the idea (though not always the term) has been more influential in theology ever since. For Otto, God is transcendent, "holy"; God's realm is the "numinous," and God is "wholly other" than humankind. IF people have any significant experience of God, the experience is one of *mysterium tremendum*—typically characterized by awe and wonder (and perhaps dread or terror), as well as by remarkable vitality, passion, spiritual power, and supreme fascination. Otto claimed, "This mental state is *sui generis* and irreducible to any other"; it is suprarational and therefore cannot be understood in rational categories.

Otto contrasted our capacity for significant religious experience with our sexuality, which "lies just on the opposite side of 'reason,' to the numinous consciousness; for, while *our capacity for sublimity is 'above all reason,'* the sex impulse is below it, an element in our instinctive life. 'The numinous' infuses the rational from above, 'the sexual' presses up from beneath, quite wholesomely and normally out of the nature which the human being shares with the general animal world."[53]

Furthermore, the two experiences—our sexuality from below and the numinous from above—cannot be sufficiently expressed in language. So communicators, from poets to artists to theologians, can only point toward and perhaps facilitate religious experience.

An approach to communicating the sublime can, to some extent, be taught, but Otto believed that the experience of the numinous could not really be taught. We can, however, "cooperate with this process" and thereby increase the possibility of people experiencing the sublime. In Otto's lexicon, "sublime" is a category from aesthetics, whereas *mysterium tremendum* refers to religious experience per se. Otto's strongly suggests, however, that the sublime experiences that are sometimes possible through great art, music, and other artful human expressions can evoke the experience of the numinous. Otto observes, "A feeling, no less than an idea, can arouse its like in the mind; and the presence of the one in my consciousness may be the occasion for my entertaining the other at the same time."[54] Otto reflects upon the record of Isaiah's call experience (in Isaiah 6) as a case of the numinous mediated through the sublime.

Postmodern thinkers, who have followed the Romantics in generally rejecting the Enlightenment's hyperrationalism and scientism, have often observed a widespread hunger for imaginal and emotional experience. They have pioneered a focus upon subjectivity and socially constructed perceptions of reality, so they have understandably elevated sublimity theory into a new prominence. **Jean-François Lyotard** famously observed in *The Postmodern Condition* that postenlightenment, postmodern people view "all metanarratives" with "incredulity." In the postmodern era, with less certitude and more pluralism and diversity, with shrinking stability and stampeding complexity, people have become remarkably more open to mystery, to the supernatural, and to experiences of transcendence.

Lyotard assigned to artists and writers the task of connecting with the human community for the sake of "healing it"—by making sublime aesthetic experience available for the masses. Lyotard featured Marcel Proust and James Joyce as writers who engaged postmodern people through "allusion." "Joyce allows the unpresentable to become perceptible in his writing. . . . It is our business not to supply reality but to invent allusions to the conceivable which cannot be presented. . . . Let us be witnesses to the unpresentable."[55]

Michael Osborn, a contemporary rhetorical theorist, has employed Martin Luther King Jr.'s "I Have a Dream" speech to update the theory of the sublime. Osborn believes that the theory substantially explains the mystery of "great speaking." He believes that the following explanations help account for the sublime impact that communicators sometimes achieve in the audience's experience.[56]

1. The communicator's very high credibility with the audience is probably a prerequisite to the experience. As Longinus observed, "Sublimity is the echo of a great soul."

2. The speaker embodies an "elevation of mind." Great ideas are intrinsically involved in sublime experience.

3. The structure of discourse contributes to the sublime effect. Osborn believes, "The speech must seem to build as it progresses, to rise to some height of insight and emotion as it carries its audience along with it." For instance, Osborn perceives "four movements" in King's address: (a) King positioned the moment in historical perspective; (b) he named and described the injustices that made the Civil Rights movement and the specific occasion necessary; (c) he shared his vision of the future that is possible; and (d) "he virtually commanded his vision to be fulfilled."

4. The speaker draws from and amplifies precedents, ideas, and opportunities that are already present in the audience and in the context, such as King's

commemoration of the nation's past; his drawing from the guarantees in the people's Constitution, from the nation's known promises to all of its people, and from the values already clear to many auditors; and the dynamics of the speech's immediate setting—a vast audience gathered at the Lincoln Memorial at a crisis time in the nation's history.

5. The speaker employs what Cicero and Augustine called the "grand style" in language and delivery. The speaker employs the figures of speech that produce the bold imagery that arouses the people's imaginations. Bold, concrete images can catalyze what Longinus called a "superior force," with which "we are drawn away from argument pure and simple to any startling image within whose dazzling brilliancy the argument lies concealed."[57]

6. The speech "transports" the audience. As Longinus wrote, "The effect of elevated language upon audience is not persuasion, but transport.... Sublimity flashing forth at the right moment scatters everything before it like a thunderbolt, and at once displays the power of the orator in all of its fullness."[58]

7. The speech extends a "great challenge" to the audience.

8. Partly as a consequence of all of this, sublime speech can give audiences a kind of "rebirth," in which (a) they see the world in a different way; (b) they discover a new identity and purpose, from which they engage in new actions; and (c) (in Longinus's words) the experience "implants in our souls the unconquerable love of whatever is elevated and more divine than we."

Compared to the Roman Catholic, Orthodox, and Anglican Christians on one side of us, and to the Pentecostals on another side, the people's experiences of Protestant Christianity do not often move them deeply, much less profoundly; our ecstasy deficit is long-standing and entrenched, and we accept it as part of "normal" Christianity. The sublime tradition invites us to rediscover the long-neglected power in imaginative, indigenous, aesthetic, elevated expression, and to reaffirm the role of great ideas, eloquently expressed and ecstatically experienced, as we consider the forms of expression in which the gospel can engage our generation. One day, we will know if the Protestant churches responded to this opportunity, because Longinus left us with this test: "That is really great which bears a repeated examination, and which it is difficult or rather impossible to withstand, and the memory of which is strong and hard to efface."[59]

CHAPTER FOUR

WHEN WE REACH OUT, WHOM WILL WE REACH?

Once a church's people understand that they are stewards of the gospel not for the their private enjoyment or to "protect" the gospel from pagans, and once a church has rediscovered that Christianity's main business is to make the life of faith, hope, and love a live option for all the people it can, and once the church has decided to pay the price of moving "from tradition to mission" to become a more apostolic congregation, one palpable question usually surfaces: "Who will we reach?"

The quandary behind the question is understandable. As this is being written, I am consulting with Pastor Debbie Wallace-Padgett and the core leader team of Saint Luke United Methodist Church in Lexington, Kentucky, a city of 400,000. Saint Luke is a visible regional church located on a main traffic artery and near another in the eastern region of the city. A pin map showing where Saint Luke's members live might reveal that 80 percent of the church's active members live in the church's natural "ministry area," a region of the city populated by 130,000 people. Well over half of those people are not actively involved in any church.[1] We estimate that Saint Luke *could* reach *at least* 5,000 of those people *if* the church could identify them and offer the possibility to them in appropriate ways over sufficient time.

Within a sea of faces, however, how does a congregation perceive the "harvest" that the Spirit is calling the church to enter, care for, and gather? Although a Church Growth text cannot prescribe as specifically as, perhaps, "Invite the Williams couple on Cedar Avenue to attend the marriage enrichment retreat," we are now confident of three clusters of answers to this indispensable strategic question.

Some Church Leaders Already Know Some of the Answers

Some of the folk wisdom that is already in the minds of some churches' leaders is enough, if implemented, for most churches to experience new growth. Although folk wisdom is usually a mixed bag of truth, half-truth, and illusion, the field research of Church Growth people has confirmed some of the strategic perspectives we sometimes hear in churches, especially in growing churches.

1. Respond to Your Visitors

When local unchurched people unilaterally visit on Sunday morning, that is seldom an impulsive, spontaneous, or random behavior like stopping to pick up ice cream or dropping by the library to peruse the new fiction. The body language of their sudden presence in church is sending "messages" for church leaders who have the eyes to see; questions, issues, needs, and even crises are often present but not yet spoken.

So strategic churches take an intentional and redundant approach in responding to visitors. (a) They make doubly sure, through attendance registration pads and usher-initiated conversations before and after the service, to get a visitor's name and contact information. (b) The church welcomes them and gives them a visitor's packet before they leave the church and someone visits, calls, or e-mails them that afternoon and perhaps again before the next Sunday. (c) In measurable time, one or more people from the church get in conversation with them and invite them to a class, a small group, a special ministry, or an event.

2. Engage Unchurched People in Your Members' Networks

Donald McGavran's early Church Growth field research revealed that the kinship and friendship networks of the people of God provide "the bridges of God"; the faith does not usually spread most naturally and contagiously to strangers but rather to the people who are connected to the church's believers—especially to the church's most credible disciples in whom relatives, friends, and neighbors can perceive changed life and authenticity. Once, churches were *not* conversant with this principle, and they believed that contacting strangers (say, at street corners or door-to-door) was "*the* way to do evangelism." But the first generation of Church Growth teaching, in the 1970s and 1980s, liberated many churches from this myth and established the "relational evangelism" paradigm within serious churches. Consequently, some churches regularly and systematically contact and invite every pre-Christian friend and relative of every member.

3. Reach Out across the Networks of Your Newest Members and Converts

This insight also is now part of Church Growth's enduring legacy. Once, evangelical Christianity experienced this as a very counterintuitive idea. New converts, they believed, were vulnerable to "outsiders," and their beliefs and lifestyle were not yet theologically and spiritually formed; so evangelism, they reasoned, is best done by our most mature and theologically informed people. McGavran displaced that paradigm in the minds of many of the church leaders who were most serious about reaching people. Many church leaders are now clear that as a group our newest converts are our best evangelizers.

New converts often make good evangelizers for several reasons: (a) New disciples still have many more contacts with pre-Christian people than long-established members have. (b) They still remember what it was like to try to make sense of one's life without Jesus Christ as Lord; many longtime members have forgotten. (c) Their faces and lives still reflect the contagion of a new discovery; many friends and relatives knew them "BC." (d) They have not yet had time to become linguistically corrupted by theologians and preachers; they still understand and speak the language of the secular marketplace. So, for such reasons, growing churches often have a very intentional, deliberate, ongoing practice of reaching out to people in the networks of their newest members and Christians.

4. Get in Ministry and Conversation with Pre-Christian People

Occasionally, the most prolific churches are "out ahead" of the other churches AND Church Growth theorists, as in this strategic principle: First *get in ministry with pre-Christian people, then get in conversation with them, and then include God in the conversation.* The most effective churches have known that lost people are much more than "souls with ears." Seekers typically have needs that can be met better through some service or ministry, or through group life or a relationship with a Christian friend, than through verbal witness alone. Besides, ministry also "communicates." When a church's people care enough to minister to people in the throes of addiction, to teach English to expatriates, to pray over a couple's premature baby, or to support someone in their loss or grief, that communicates volumes and gives credibility to what we say in the gospel's service.

So strategic churches typically act in two strategic ways: (a) They discover and invite all the people they can find who could be served through the church's present range of ministries. (b) They develop new *outreach ministries* to serve and reach additional populations. Some churches now feature 50 or more lay-led outreach ministries, and they are unstoppable local movements.

5. Identify the Types of People for Whom You Have a Heart

Many churches grow as they *identify the specific populations they have a heart for,* and they develop new outreach ministries, classes, fellowships, and congregations to engage and disciple those people.[2] So one finds churches now reaching, for example, people who are deaf, gambling addicts, single-parent families, people with mental illnesses, or Laotian immigrant people because a team of people within the church began following their hearts. Churches often experience more growth from such ministries than they expected. For instance, a church that begins ministry with the Deaf may find they are also reaching the families of the Deaf *and* many other people who are attracted to a church that cares enough to minister to people who are deaf.

6. Reach People Who Are Like Your Active Members

Many churches know that *people who are like their active members will be more responsive than people who are very different.* Donald McGavran's discovery of the realities behind his "homogeneous unit principle" (that most pre-Christian people find response to the gospel more possible when they are not required to cross major language, ethnic, cultural, or class barriers to become Christians) essentially ratified what many church leaders already knew: social barriers are often more formidable than theological barriers to initial entry into the church and faith. Most churches do not, in policy or practice, intend to exclude anyone, but, as a practical matter, they do not usually invite people who are illiterate to attend a participatory Bible study, or people who are deaf to attend an unsigned service, or non-English speakers to visit an English-language congregation.

So a specific congregation reaches, most often, the kind of people that the congregation already engages most effectively. Many churches, however, no longer limit their local mission to the people that one relatively homogeneous congregation already understands and knows how to serve; the church "proliferates" groups, fellowships, ministries, and congregations to reach people of subcultures, cultures, and language groups beyond what one congregation alone could reach. In time, those groups and congregations become best at reaching people like them, and so on. The relatively heterogeneous growing church is a constellation of relatively homogeneous groups, ministries, and congregations.

The Church Growth Movement's Biggest Answer: Reach Receptive People

Whereas Church Growth researchers have confirmed, or once introduced, the strategic lore that now drives many growing churches, Donald McGavran once featured and unpacked a very major strategic theme that is no longer prominent in the thinking of many church leaders today. It was prominent in their predecessors' minds a quarter century ago and it led to expansion in their time, and it drives some world mission agencies today, but it was not passed on in the socialization of most of today's church leaders. When leaders do learn the principle, however, and take it seriously, they typically identify more reachable people than they can get to. The principle can be stated in one sentence: *Identify, and reach out to, the people who are most likely to be receptive.*

We are already familiar with this principle at the common-sense level. A teenager, for example, waits until *after* dinner (when Dad will be more receptive) to ask for the family car for Friday evening; a suitor "pops the question" when he senses it is the right time; when a salesperson senses that the shopper has almost decided, she asks, "Shall I wrap it up?" The field of marketing helps organizations identify, understand, and engage the people who would be most interested in their product or service. One of Shakespeare's characters famously observed, "There is a tide in the affairs of men, which taken at the flood, leads on to fortune; omitted, all the voyage of their life is bound in shallows and in miseries" (*Julius Caesar*, IV.iii.218-19). The faith that is rooted in the incarnation also extends in ways that are consistent with these natural patterns of people and societies. So Jesus admonished his disciples to "look around" and see where "the fields are ripe for harvesting" (John 4:35).

Evangelization also depends, however, on supernatural dynamics. The Holy Spirit, working through the events and circumstances of some people's lives in every season, is creating a "harvest" for God's church to gather. Our role is to discern where and in whom the Spirit is working. And if, through our outreach, ministry, and witness, the penny drops and the bell rings, and they discover the gift of faith, this too is primarily the Holy Spirit's work; we are merely the midwives in the miracle of second birth. Because circumstances change in people's lives, and because the Holy Spirit "blows where [the Holy Spirit] wills," receptivity ebbs and flows in the lives of people and peoples. Some people are more receptive now than they were a year ago; some are less receptive. Donald McGavran reflected:

> Fluctuating receptivity is a most prominent aspect of human nature and society.... The receptivity or responsiveness of individuals waxes and wanes. No person is equally ready at all times to follow "the Way."...Peoples and societies also vary in responsiveness. Whole segments of mankind resist the Gospel for periods—often very long periods—and then ripen to the Good News....Missions in Africa, Asia, and Latin America also abundantly illustrate the fact that societies ripen to the Gospel at different times....Sudden

ripenings, far from being unusual, are common. . . . One thing is clear—receptivity wanes as often as it waxes. Like the tide, it comes in and goes out. Unlike the tide, no one can guarantee when it goes out that it will soon come back again.[3]

This last reality is a source of "apostolic urgency." When the harvest is ready, we must gather it before it spoils, lest we miss the day of their visitation, and they spend the rest of their lives "in shallows."

◆　　◆　　◆　　◆

Church Growth's major *strategic* contribution to churches, through extensive field research among growing churches and Christian movements, has been the identification of major *indicators* of probable receptivity in people. Repeatedly we have observed that certain things are going on in people's lives before or during the time they open to the gospel.

7. A Population in Which Any Religion, Philosophy, or Ideology Is Spreading May Be Receptive

When, for example, a church finds people who read their daily horoscope with some seriousness, the church should *not* assume that astrology will meet the deepest needs of their souls or will maintain its influence upon them forever; they are currently anxious about the future and the gospel of hope can meet that need profoundly.

8. A Population in Which Any Religion, Philosophy, or Ideology Is Declining May Be Receptive

For example, following the implosion of Soviet Communism in the early 1990s, many of the peoples of eastern Europe were receptive and many missions planted many churches; that receptivity has waned in recent years.

9. Population Mobility Induces Widespread Receptivity

When people pick up roots and move to another land (or region) and culture, they are typically open to new friendships, alliances, ideas, roots, and possibilities for their lives. The general term *mobility* obscures some important distinctions. Refugees, immigrants, expatriates, new residents from within the same nation, and even foreign students typically have very contrasting experiences, and they need to be approached in ways that engage their respective needs; but all five groups are usually much more receptive than they were where they came from.

10. Many People in a Changing Culture Will Be Receptive

So, for example, when the culture's traditional values are no longer nailed down, when traditional beliefs or attitudes are changing, when aesthetic tastes and musical preferences are changing, when traditional institutions are failing, or the culture's economics or politics are volatile, many people are open to turning to the God who is "the same yesterday, today, and forever." Many American churches have discovered, for instance, that the same generation that would not buy their fathers' Oldsmobile will not buy their fathers' church; this appears to be the most important single insight driving the "emergent churches."

11. People in Christians' Networks Will Usually Be More Receptive than Strangers

This principle relates to the second and third principles, above—that churches grow as they reach out across the social networks of their people, especially their newest converts—but it adds a reason for emphasizing network outreach: the people who are linked to our most credible Christians, who see life-change and authenticity in them, will be much more responsive to the church than the general population will be.

12. If You Can Minister to Their Needs, They May Be Receptive

Increasingly, churches first get in ministry with people in response to some need, struggle, or issue in their lives, and then they get in conversation with the people, and then they include God in the conversation. They do this in two ways.

- They identify an existing ministry that already meets the needs of people in the church, and they offer it to people with the same need who are outside the church. One church, for instance, made its "Mother's Day Out" program more widely available.

- They develop a new outreach ministry in response to an underserved population in the ministry area. A church in Las Vegas, for instance, developed a new twelve-step ministry for people with a gambling addiction.

13. People Who Are Dissatisfied with Their Lives May Be Receptive

This would appear to be the most generic of the guidelines. Most satisfied people, in general, are not looking for change; but dissatisfied people are more likely to be open to change. Dissatisfaction with one's *life* fundamentally amplifies the dynamics of receptivity; many such people become not only open, but active seekers. For many people, their dreams have not been fulfilled or their lives have not turned out as they once imagined; they know there must be "something more," that life was meant to be more than they have experienced. Many people cannot affirm the person who looks back from the mirror when they comb their hair each morning. Many such people will be open to the adventurous, meaningful, abundant life of the Christ-follower, if we interpret it and offer it.

14. People Experiencing Transition Are More Receptive than People in Stability

We are now reasonably sure of the life transitions that often induce receptivity, although we cannot with mathematical precision say that one transition induces twice as much as another. Many people become more receptive during and following certain transitions that virtually everyone experiences, such as adolescence, leaving home for college or work, marriage, birth of the first child, the last child leaving home, retirement, or loss of a close relative or friend to death. Other transitions that many people experience also induce receptivity, such as promotion or termination, separation or divorce, second marriage or retirement. Many churches, as one example, offer support groups and "Beginning Again" seminars for people in the throes of divorce.

◆　　　◆　　　◆　　　◆

Although Church Growth people counsel churches to identify and reach receptive people, we are *not* called to abandon indifferent or resistant people. McGavran taught church leaders to maintain "a light loving presence" among resistant people—loving and serving them as much as they will let us, saying what we can, knowing that we are thereby "planting seeds" that may grow into a harvest in God's good time. Nevertheless, we are called to win the winnable while they are winnable, and mission agencies should even redeploy many of their mission personnel to the most receptive fields.

Postscript: In consultations and training events with several congregations, I have discovered that the harvest metaphor can be misinterpreted (especially in city churches) to promise something like "instant new members." The following analogy helps suggest the actual reality. Receptive people are something like the very "scheduled" young woman I once knew who had completed her education and had paid off her education debts, and was now well placed in her first professional role. She was now, at last, open to marriage and starting a family. That new openness did *not* mean that she would have accepted a first-date marriage proposal! It did mean that she was now open to the kind of relationship she had been closed to before. It would still take some time and shared dating history for her and any interesting man to construct together the kind of relationship that would warrant the step into marriage. I am suggesting that there are probably no more instant members than there are instant marriage partners. Once people become receptive, the process that moves them toward crossing over to the Christian side typically takes a season or two.

For Strategic Reasons, Target These Populations Too

15. Target the Masses More than the Classes

Donald McGavran was sure that most missions should *target the masses more than the classes*. This principle contrasts with the practice of most missions. For most of mission history, missionaries have been understandably attracted to engaging the educated professional nationals who were most like the missionaries; reach the classes, they believed, and the Christian movement will "percolate" down to the masses. The usual problem, however, has been that the classes were much less receptive than the masses, and so the movement was often stillborn at the top. McGavran and other students of mission have observed that most Christian movements actually begin lower on the socioeconomic scale, sometimes with people who have very little status or power in their society, and from their converts the movement spreads out and up.

Eugene Nida expanded upon this insight with more precision.[4] Nida observed, as a cultural anthropologist, that most societies have six classes of people—based on factors like ancestry, wealth, education, and talent. In an astonishing expression of academic clarity, Nida named these classes:

The upper upper class

The lower upper class

The upper middle class

The lower middle class

The upper lower class

The lower lower class

The percentage of a society's people in each class will vary from one society to another; most of Haiti's people are in the lower lower class; the majority of Uruguay's are upper middle class. Which of those factors counts most in determining one's class will vary from one society to another; ancestry, for instance, weighs much more heavily in India's caste society than in England's more porous, but still class-conscious, society. The degree of vertical mobility that is possible will vary from one society to another; most Indians are stuck in the caste into which they were born, while moving up the scale is enormously more possible in Canada.

The reflections of Nida and McGavran combine to offer a cluster of astonishingly useful insights.

- While most missions try to begin with the upper classes, most Protestant Christian *movements* begin by reaching people in the target society's lower middle class and, especially, the upper lower class.

- The movement spreads, sometimes contagiously, as they reach their peers.

- In time, as the converts, for example, are liberated from demon rum and spousal abuse, as their self-esteem rises and they face the future with more hope, as they become literate and their children acquire educations, as they acquire discipline and plan their lives, as they gain church leadership experience and a changed worldview, they experience "redemption and lift"; they move up the social ladder.

- In time, however, they are cut off from the social ranks out of which they emerged. They no longer "speak the language" of the people they came from, they no longer have living contacts among them, and they have forgotten how to reach them. Sometimes the people left behind resent them.

At this point, McGavran observed, Christian movements plateau—their growth graph levels off and, in time, the movement starts to decline and is no longer a movement. McGavran featured only one major way to continue to reach the lower classes: continually start "new work" among them.

16. Target the Heads of Families and Clans

Since the biblical period, churches have often grown by targeting and reaching the patriarchs or matriarchs of extended families. When they are discipled, they provide an influential bridge to every other family member. If enough family members are reached, their self-defined shared identity changes. They are now a Christian family or clan, providing in-family support for every Christian in the family and passing on the faith to the next generation.

17. Target the Wider Social Unit's Opinion Leaders

The "diffusion of innovations" school of thought has demonstrated that new ideas, practices, products, services, and technologies, in all societies and smaller social units, spread through the people who monitor trends and opportunities in the wider world AND are looked to as "influencers" within their group; no new possibility would stand much of a chance without their recommendation. In the Middle Ages, Christianity likewise spread through the influence of kings, queens, barons, nobles, and other people of recognized influence. The approach began early. Michael Green tells us in *Evangelism in the Early Church* that

> Paul...seems to have made a deliberate policy of going for leaders in a community, through whom, if he were successful in bringing them to Christian commitment, the message might be widely disseminated.... These men were of no more intrinsic value to God than any beggar in the streets; but their influence, if converted, was infinitely greater.[5]

18. Target Nonreligious People

This rather obvious option does not occur to most Christians. When they think about evangelization, they think about evangelizing Hindus, Muslims, Buddhists, or devotees of some other religious tradition or of another Christian denomination. The research of sociologist Rodney Stark reveals, however,

> People who are deeply committed to any particular faith do not go out and join some other faith.... Converts to new religious movements are overwhelmingly from relatively irreligious backgrounds.... New Religious Movements mainly draw their converts from the ranks of the religiously inactive and discontented."[6]

Some churches have lived by this focus. Chicago's Willow Creek Community Church has long defined its mission as helping "irreligious people become fully devoted followers of Jesus Christ."

19. Target People with the Talents, Resources, or Contacts That Your Movement Will Need

When Redeemer Presbyterian Church decided to feature a jazz congregation to engage Manhattan's considerable population of jazz lovers, the church did not have enough jazz musicians to form a jazz band. So a team of people visited the jazz clubs, recruiting musicians—some believers, some not yet believers.

20. Target the "Impossible" People

The establishment in every society, it seems, writes off some types of people; they are, by socially agreed definition, "hopeless," "impossible," or "losers." The church, tragically, has too often shared such appraisals from the surrounding society. As I demonstrate in *The Celtic Way of Evangelism* and in *Radical Outreach*, apostolic movements typically begin with the opposite assumption—that, because of what Charles Wesley called "the wideness of God's mercy," many of the "impossible" people can be reached and, as some of them experience such great life-change that the society perceives them as "miracles," this catalyzes such wider receptivity in the whole society that a Christian movement becomes possible.

This dynamic helped launch the very earliest Christian movement. For instance, in the first-century Hebrew society reflected in the pages of the New Testament, what did the following groups of people have in common: lepers; people who were blind or deaf; people who were physically disabled, possessed, or mentally ill; Samaritans; prostitutes; zealots; tax collectors; and others? They were all prohibited from entering the Temple. Most readers will recall that much of Jesus' ministry was to the officially hopeless people of the society. (That was, partly, what got him crucified!) This wide redemptive perspective did not escape the notice of the disciples who became apostles. In the wider Mediterranean world, most of them reached so-called barbarian populations; a couple of apostles reached cannibal populations. So Ted Turner is actually half right in his famous charge, "Christianity is a religion for losers." Our very long experience would suggest that Christianity represents the only power in the cosmos that can change "losers" into "winners."

Postscript: On Getting Your Apostolic Act Together

Many of the people who began reading this chapter, hoping to know "who to reach," may now feel overwhelmed by the twenty suggestions that the chapter unpacked. The last section, for instance, counsels churches to target the masses, heads of families and clans, opinion leaders within social units, nonreligious people, "impossible" people, and people with needed talents, and so forth. Which of *those* many people should we reach? We conclude with two answers to that question:

- Look for the most *receptive* of those people, using the guidelines in the previous section.

- *Pray* that the Lord of the Harvest will *lead* you to the people God has prepared for your church to reach.

CHAPTER FIVE

EVANGELIZING PRE-CHRISTIAN PEOPLE: A THEMATIC PERSPECTIVE

Christian leaders are called to love "the Lord of the Harvest" with mind and heart. In our Christian traditions, believers affirm some people in leadership roles because, in part, they seem to understand and articulate the tradition's folk wisdom best, and they seem to have the combination of spirituality and street smarts needed to lead the churches into the future that God wills.[1] New leaders, however, too often assume that our tradition's folk wisdom is enough, or they assume that they know as much as the people think they do! Some leaders even assume their own (or their peer group's or their tradition's) infallibility!

Our capacity to actually lead churches and Christian movements, however, is limited by the intelligence that informs our strategic decisions. Computer geeks tell us, "Garbage in, garbage out"; the outputs can be no better than the inputs. The intelligence that can inform strategic thinking is acquired through learning and discovery. The discoveries usually come from asking the right questions and, like drilling for oil, from asking and drilling in the right places, for long enough, for the insights to emerge. Donald McGavran's career stands as an enduring model of this principle.

McGavran especially dared to ask the big question that most church leaders had ignored for generations because they had already agreed on the answers! *How* does the church do evangelism *effectively*? McGavran discovered that all most leaders knew for sure was their socially constructed consensus on how new people *ought* to be reached and how churches *should* grow.[2] McGavran observed that often the approach or plan a company of people has agreed upon *might not* be informed by the valid intelligence that would be necessary for navigating the future they desire. He observed that churches that based their local mission upon evangelical folk wisdom usually walked out of ripe harvest fields empty-handed.

So, when McGavran was a mission leader in India in the 1930s, superintending many churches whose leaders said they were doing "evangelism" but were not actually reaching pre-Christian people, he began asking, "How does the gospel *actually* spread? How do churches *really* grow?" In 1934, from a three-year field-research study of what came to be called India's "people movements" into Christianity, J. Waskom Pickett published a pioneering text. In the Indian Christian newspaper *Sahayak Patrika*, McGavran published a review of Pickett's book. You can infer by his opening sentence that he liked the book: "There has come a book sent by God, and its name is *Christian Mass Movements in India*." With his background in behavioral sciences and field research in his PhD studies at Columbia University, McGavran brought a perceptive mind to appraise Pickett's project.

As McGavran studied the book and then spent a month with Pickett studying growing churches, he became convinced that mission's conceptual frontiers could no longer draw from Scripture, mission history, and theology *alone*. The complexity of mission's challenge also required *field research*. We needed to study enough growing churches and Christian movements, in enough tongues and cultures, to determine what growing churches *know* and what they *do* (that other churches do not know and do) to reach people, and grow, and become local Christian movements. Such churches and movements can model the way forward for other churches. In churches that are growing with integrity and power, the God who acts in history is revealing the reproducible or adaptable *principles* that can inform the Christian movement's expansion elsewhere.

So, in sabbaticals and supported by occasional research grants, McGavran studied growing churches on four continents over a twenty-year period. He studied their growth history; he observed their ministries; he interviewed leaders and converts; and, in time, he could describe universal patterns that account for Christianity's expansion, presumably everywhere. McGavran's reflection, however, could be *prescriptive*, as well as descriptive. From the New Testament, he challenged the prevailing understanding that the *goal* of evangelism was to "get decisions." From the Great Commission in Matthew 28 and from the ministry modeled in the Acts of the Apostles, McGavran taught that evangelism's goal is to "make disciples," not merely to elicit decisions. Disciples, he taught, *follow Jesus Christ as Lord*, in the church and in the world.

Stephen Neill, the Anglican missionary statesman, used to similarly nuance the goals of evangelism in terms of the New Testament word *metanoia*, and he contended that God wants and the world needs the kinds of Christian disciples who have experienced three "turnings." People are called to turn (1) to Christ, (2) to the body of Christ, and (3) to a vision of the kind of world that Christ wants—in terms like *life*, *justice*, and *peace*. Neill's model becomes especially useful with two additional observations: (1) These three turnings typically take place *one at a time* in a person's life; and (2) they occur *in any conceivable sequence*. (Bishop Neill used to reflect that most of the "useless" Christians were people in whom one or two of the turnings had been experienced, but not yet all three. Furthermore, in evangelism we are called to invite people into any of the three turnings they have not yet experienced.)

An interest in Stephen Neill's third turning is more in ascendancy than ever before. In many places where evangelical Christianity has grown substantially, from Asia to Africa to Latin America, church leaders confess that, although their churches have grown, their societies have not changed. More leaders are now clear that God wants God's will to be done "on earth, as it is in heaven." So George Otis (www. sentinelgroup.org) produces books and videos dramatizing where transformations are taking place. Donald Miller and Tetsunao Yamamori document how Pentecostal Christianity is developing a greater social conscience.[3] Pete Wagner, who did his PhD in ethics, has recently published *Dominion: How Kingdom Action Can Change the World*.[4] (The new evangelical desire for Christian influence in social reform is not a new discovery, but rather a *rediscovery* of the vision that inspired the nineteenth-century abolitionist movement.)

The history of an evangelical understanding of *how* we work for a new world may soon parallel the history of our understanding of evangelism. Once, as in the first Great Awakening, we were clearer about God's role in saving people than we were about the church's role. McGavran and the Church Growth school discovered more about what *we* do to cooperate with the Great Commission than we ever knew before. Today, evangelicals are clearer about what God does in social reform, and most of our efforts (such as organized intercession) are related to the divine side. One day scholars will do the field research in churches that are making a social difference, to discover the reproducible principles behind the human side of Christian social engagement.

We are already clearer than before about one goal of evangelism: while we are, indeed, called to join the Lord in making citizens of heaven, we are also called to join God in making the kind of Christian citizens for the world that the world needs, in great numbers, to populate the movements that will make a difference.

◆ ◆ ◆ ◆

In time, other field researchers and interpreters joined Donald McGavran in what became the Church Growth Movement. Such studies, however, were not confined to Church Growth people. In time, a number of behavioral scientists studied some of the same issues.[5] Christian conversion has particularly been studied from several useful vantage points.[6] Some scholars, notably Lyle Schaller, have studied churches with interests very similar to those of Church Growth people.[7]

This chapter addresses McGavran's formidable question: *How* does effective evangelism actually take place?[8] We have, today, advanced some beyond McGavran's strategic wisdom. In this chapter, his most significant single principle will be sandwiched third among four strategic principles that can now be drawn from broader and later research. (To aid the reader's memory, I have imposed alliteration upon the four principles.)

Community

Apostolic outreach is prepared for, takes place within, and is deployed from the several forms of Christian community. As John Wesley famously observed, "Christianity is not a solitary religion." Some Christian leaders, in some generations, have known this since Jesus gathered twelve disciples and shaped them into the symbolic New Israel. The research and reflection behind my book on ancient Celtic Christianity and that movement's approach to mission helped me drill deeper in understanding this principle.[9]

The Celtic Christian movement's people were substantially reached by, formed within, and deployed from Christian communities. The Celtic Christian movement lasted from the fifth to the ninth centuries and was the greatest sustained Christian mission in Christianity's history. The movement reached many of the peoples of what are now Ireland, Scotland, and England, and, in time, reached many peoples of western Europe. Their mission was widely assumed to be impossible to achieve because Rome perceived as "barbarians" the populations that the movement targeted; by definition, people had to be sufficiently "civilized" to become Christianized. By achieving the "impossible," the Celtic Christian movement brought Europe out of the Dark Ages and ushered in a thousand years of (more or less) Christian culture in Europe. Their achievement is unexplainable apart from the contagious power of Christian community in several forms.

In the late fourth century, Patrick grew up in a Briton tribe in what is now northwest England. He was raised in a Christian family and in the local church, and he learned the catechism—though he had not accepted the faith (and had rebelled against it) when, as a teenager, he was captured by pirates and sold into slavery in Ireland. As a slave, he lived much of the time in the compound with other slaves next to the tribal settlement of an Irish leader named Milieuc. In other periods, Patrick experienced isolation while he was herding cattle in a wilderness area miles from the settlement.

In the compound, there were undoubtedly Christian slaves who formed into Christian community and included Patrick in their company, praying with and for him. The community of faith back home was praying for him, and Patrick now carried vivid memories of that community within him. In the wilderness periods, he began praying more and more. In time, he became aware of the presence of God, and he recognized this presence to be the Triune God he had learned about in the catechism. Patrick experienced the gift of faith and became devout. At the settlement, his fellow Christians and his captors observed profound change within him.

Patrick, after six years of life in slavery and now in his early twenties, escaped on a ship and returned to England. He acquired a theological education and served for two decades as a parish priest. In a dream years later, at the age of forty-eight, he experienced a "Macedonian call" to take the gospel to the Irish. With the support of England's bishops and Pope Celestine, Patrick attracted and trained an "apostolic band" to join him in a mission to the Irish. In (or about) A.D. 432, the band sailed for Ireland and made its way inland to Saul, where they planted the first church of the Christian movement in Ireland.

Patrick served as an "apostle to the Irish" for the next twenty-eight years. By the time of his death in A.D 470, the movement had reached at least forty of Ireland's 150 tribes. Within the next two generations, all of Ireland was substantially reached, and so in one century Ireland changed from the least Christianized to the most Christianized area in the Roman Empire. This achievement came through, and not without, the power of Christian community and through the astonishing proliferation of Christian communities and types of Christian communities.

Their basic early outreach pattern saw the apostolic band setting up camp next to an unreached settlement—befriending the people; getting in ministry and conversation with the people; inviting the more receptive people into the band's fellowship and, in time, raising up a new church in the settlement; and then moving on to replicate the process in the next settlement over. In time, the movement proliferated other apostolic bands, which made it possible to reach more settlements. So they proliferated bands that proliferated congregations.

At some point, probably while Patrick still lived, the movement learned from the monasteries of the eastern church, which they adapted into a new form of Christian community for the western church. In the east, people escaped from the world, and from perceived corruptions in the church, into the monasteries—to save their souls.

Now in the west, by comparison, people joined the monastic communities to prepare to extend the church and to save other people's souls. Their purpose in what is now called "Celtic spirituality" was to form people for ministry and mission. While the monastic communities were preparing Christians, they were also receiving pre-Christian seekers into the life of their community. Indeed, the ministry to seekers within the monastic community helped prepare people for ministry and witness beyond.[10]

The monastic communities proliferated other kinds of communities for reaching and building people.

- They invented a new form of dyad—a group of two people in which one person was the seeker or the newer Christian and the other was his or her "soul friend." One's soul friend was not a superior but was someone with whom one was willing to be vulnerable and accountable.
- They invented a form of small group—a dozen or so people whose leader was recognized as devout. Everyone met in their small group in which they were in ministry with one another and with any seeker in their ranks.
- They proliferated worshiping congregations within the monastic community AND within the churches they planted. The maximum length of the available lumber in Ireland did not permit them to build churches to accommodate more than perhaps fifty or sixty people at a time; so that fact forced what, in any case, would have been their inclination. The monastic communities and the churches in settlements proliferated congregations from the beginning.
- In each season, they were preparing multiple apostolic teams to reach the settlements in their region. (The bands consisted of a dozen or so people; they assumed that Jesus probably got the number about right!)
- The apostolic teams (or bands) moved out to plant churches in every settlement. The churches, in turn, proliferated congregations, small groups, and ministries.

Celtic Christianity's penchant for community was not, of course, the sole reason for the movement's expansion. (Church Growth is *never* sufficiently explained by a single cause.) The movement was culturally relevant. It departed from Rome's mandate to do church "the Roman way" everywhere; it adapted to the local population's language, culture, and aesthetics, virtually everywhere. The movement was emotionally relevant. Compared to the Roman left-brained, rational approach, Celtic Christianity engaged the Irish and other "barbarian" peoples as a faith of the imagination and the heart. Furthermore, in contrast to the male clericalism that characterized Roman Christianity, Celtic Christianity was essentially a lay movement AND it included laywomen (such as Brigid and Hilda) in notable leadership. But the movement's grounding in radical community especially has much to teach us. Bede (the eighth-century historian) profiles the monastic community at Whitby, founded and led by Hilda: "After the example of the primitive church, no one was rich, no one was in need, for they had all things in common and none had any private property."[11]

For Protestant evangelicals today, the most counterintuitive theme in the Celtic model calls for welcoming pre-Christian seekers into the ranks of faithful groups and congregations *before* they have experienced grace or believed much of anything; *our* usual script, today, is to welcome people *after* they confess the faith. However, some of the most significant research with converts today strongly ratifies the Celtic model. For instance, John Finney and his colleagues surveyed and interviewed hundreds of converts, in several Christian traditions, in Great Britain. In *Finding Faith Today*, they report that most converts experience the gift of faith *through* the relationships they experience *within* a community of faith. For most people, "belonging comes before believing."[12] In my own field research, I have interviewed first-generation disciples since the mid-1960s. I have usually asked, "When did you feel like you really belonged, like you were wanted and welcomed and included in the fellowship?" More than half of the boomer generation converts and at least three-quarters of the Generation X and Generation Y converts report that they felt like that *before* they joined or believed. As Western society becomes increasingly postmodern, more and more people will "belong before they believe" and, more and more, the faith be "more caught than taught."

We could easily fill a book with case studies of pioneering churches that have reached and discipled people *as* they have proliferated faith-communities, large and small. One such case will do. When Craig Groeschel was a student at Phillips Theological Seminary in Oklahoma, he dreamed of starting a new church that one day would proliferate campuses; his faculty discouraged him. Then his Oklahoma Conference of the United Methodist Church said no, the idea was not viable. The Evangelical Covenant Church made room for Groeschel's vision, however, and the rest is a history that is still unfolding.

Craig and Amy Groeschel started what became LifeChurch.tv in a rented dance studio in Edmund, Oklahoma, in 1996. Their mission, from the beginning, has been "to lead people to become fully devoted followers of Jesus Christ." Their design, from the beginning, involved (1) multiplying "LifeGroups," which would be ports of entry for many seekers and in which people would get in ministry with one another through relationships, caring, and accountability; (2) it involved multiplying congregations within the Edmund church; and (3) the vision involved the then novel idea of becoming one church with many campuses.

By the end of 2001, seven congregations on two campuses were serving 5,500 people per weekend. Three years later, they had four campuses and 16 congregations serving more than 12,000 people per weekend. By the end of 2007, they had expanded to a dozen campuses (AND an Internet campus), with 49 congregations serving more than 21,000 people per weekend. At this writing, LifeChurch's people are now meeting in more than 3,000 LifeGroups, including some groups whose people are attached to the Internet campus. The church is proactive in mission, locally and globally. The church supports missionaries in six nations on three continents. Whether the people are involved in Habitat for Humanity or some other expression of local mission, or whether they engage in short-term experiences in supporting their missions in other lands, they typically serve in *teams*.

Compassion

Most Protestant leaders virtually count on *words alone* to communicate all of the meaning that Christianity has to offer. If preaching and teaching can't get it all done, that is too bad, because that is what we were trained to do and like to do!

However, if we think about it even at the level of ordinary folk wisdom, we already know that "actions speak louder than words," and "a picture is worth a thousand words"; and when someone's actions contradict their words, or even when their inflection or facial expression suggests a different message than their words, we believe the nonverbal message more.

At a more academic level, the anthropologist Edward T. Hall discovered that *culture* is "the silent language," and that a culture's language is only one of perhaps ten "message systems" through which meaning gets communicated—though the communication takes place at a less conscious level than when we communicate through the language message system.

For instance, Hall explained that we also communicate in many ways through space and time.[13] Christianity has had some knowledge of these dimensions for a very long time. So we have found profound meaning in pilgrimages to holy places, and we often designate sacred space within our churches. We also have used the holy days and seasons of the Christian year to communicate, celebrate, and rehearse the faith's story and its towering themes. Furthermore, from the earliest Christian movement and throughout much of our history, we have often turned to sacraments, music, drama, the visual arts, and visual symbols (like the fish and the cross) to communicate in ways that transcend mere words.

All of this is preamble to one cogent affirmation: love communicates. Love, understood in the New Testament *agape* sense of "goodwill," communicates volumes. As our folk wisdom reminds us, "People don't care how much you know; they want to know how much you care."

The present state of our understanding is more nuanced than that. The movement of many people toward Christian faith follows a sequence something like this. As a rough generalization:

- People become more receptive to involvement with a church during a season of their lives when they are "between gods." They have given up on whatever they most recently relied upon to complete their lives and are open to something else.

- They are more likely to visit a church *if* they have heard about it.

- They are more likely to visit *if* the church has a positive public image.

- They are more likely to visit *if* one or more church members (whom they know and trust) invites them—perhaps several times, or more.

- When they visit, they look for clear signs of *life* or energy. Although often they cannot verbalize it, they realize they need grace or spiritual power to overcome their sins and problems, without which they cannot live new lives and become the people they were meant to be (and have always wanted to be).

77

- They look to see if there are people in the church who are like them—people who would understand them, with whom they can identify, and who might serve as role models.

- They sense whether they can relate to and make meaning from the church's language, music, style, and aesthetics.

- *If* they get this far, they are now looking to see how *committed* the people are to the church's truth claims and mission. As Dean M. Kelley once observed, most people are not epistemologically sophisticated; they cannot weigh competing truth claims about ultimate reality. So they likely believe the group that seems to believe in the group's message and cause the most and that sacrifices to advance it. (Conversely, mere church-attending nominal Christianity has *no* magnetic appeal to lost people who are trying to find the Way.) Growing churches are high-expectation churches. They expect a lot from their members, and many members rise to meet the expectations. They live by Christian disciplines AND are involved in a small group, in a lay ministry, and in evangelism and mission.[14]

- Furthermore, *if* they get this far they are by now observing how *loving* and *caring* the church is. They have heard that, whatever else Christians are supposed to be, they are people who love other people (and they often expect Christians to love nature's creatures as well). As our song affirms, "They will know we are Christians by our love."[15] People seem almost hardwired to check for what the New Testament calls *agape* love, which is defined not as a feeling, but as "goodwill on fire."

- By now, also, the church is able to engage seekers more deeply if they have perceived the church to be *credible*. In interviews, they typically comment on how the church's *consistency* (between what it believes and what the church and its people do) impressed and moved them. And they especially comment on how *compassionate* they found the church to be. To misquote Paul ever so slightly: often, of all of the factors seekers look for, "the greatest of these is love."

Specifically, a seeker's radar detects how much the church wants and cares for *them*, their families, and for people like them. I recently interviewed a couple who transferred from one church to another. They still more strongly affirmed the first church's doctrine, but their new church loved them and their handicapped child much more, and they said, "For us, that made all the difference."

Seekers are also moved when they observe churches that engage in visible *compassionate ministries* to target populations with special needs. Three examples will suffice.

1. It is almost impossible to find churches with visible ministries to the Deaf that are not growing. Seekers are typically moved when they visit a church that cares enough to sign its worship experience, and to engage in other ministries, for the

people among them who are deaf. Such churches typically reach three groups: the Deaf , their families and friends, and many other people who are attracted to a church that loves people who are deaf.

2. The Lutheran Church, Missouri Synod, attracts many people because of its remarkably organized and serious outreach to people who are blind. The denomination took seriously the fact that more than eleven million people who were blind or visually impaired were living in North America and were one of the nation's most underserved populations. They launched the Lutheran Blind Mission Society in 1994 (www.blindmission.org). Within a decade, people who were blind or visually impaired were being served with the largest Christian library of large print books, books in Braille, and cassette tapes in North America. The mission trains and equips leaders for blind ministries, and helps faith-communities of people who are blind get organized. Soon, the mission will make available to churches hymnals and liturgical service books in large print and Braille.

3. Ministry to people with addictions is perhaps the most impressive movement in North American Christianity and beyond. When two recovering addicts founded Alcoholics Anonymous in 1935, the Reverend Sam Shoemaker coached the new movement, but it was not primarily a movement within churches because of the widespread stigmatizing that alcoholics then experienced from church people. In time, the movement learned more and more about the multiple causes of addiction. As it became clear that the affliction is a disease (in the sense that diabetes and allergies are understood within the disease paradigm), the movement's usefulness and power spread to people in the grips of other chemical dependencies and to people with food and gambling addictions.

In the 1980s, more and more churches became educated in such matters, and a quiet movement within churches began spreading—building on the twelve steps of Alcoholics Anonymous while offering a more complete revelation and recovery than A. A. could. More and more churches feature and advertise recovery ministries and recovery congregations; a huge sign by a church in Chicago reads "Recovery Spoken Here!" Today, the recovery movement is the "underground awakening" of the early twenty-first century. More people are probably experiencing initial grace through this movement than through all evangelism programming combined. And, when a church reaches addicts and some experience profound life change, and the church is known for having "miracles" within its membership, this catalyzes much wider interest within the community.[16]

My colleague Bob Tuttle's flight to Orlando had landed. A man across the aisle had noticed Bob reading his Bible. The man asked, "May I tell you why I joined a church? I was working on a project in Anchorage, Alaska, and visited a church one Sunday. I noticed an attractive, well-dressed, middle-aged lady sitting on an aisle several rows ahead of me. A homeless young man entered the church. He walked down the aisle. The lady moved over and motioned for him to join her. I saw them smiling and talking together. I saw them sing together from a shared hymnal and pray together. Following the benediction, she hugged him and slipped him a bill. I approached her, and commented on the lovely way she had treated her son. She replied, 'Thanks, but he is not my son. I never saw him before.' That afternoon, I telephoned my wife and said, 'Let's move to Anchorage. I have found a church that practices what it preaches!'"[17]

Connections

Donald McGavran devoted two decades of field research in Christian movements on several continents to the big question that most church leaders had long ignored: *How* does the gospel spread? *How* does effective evangelism take place? In raising that question and in finding answers, McGavran was defying perhaps the most entrenched myth in the theological academy—that the academy should stick to theory and that considerations of "method" are beneath intellectuals, if not obscene. McGavran discovered, however, that understanding the communication of Christianity's message to pre-Christian populations—especially to different cultures and in different languages—is a more formidable intellectual challenge than most academic intellectuals ever face.

McGavran discovered that growing churches and Christian movements are very complex phenomena, and that growth is always the result of multiple causes AND the Holy Spirit moving in the peoples' hearts. The mission of Church Growth field research was to identify as many of those causes as possible. Beneath the complexity, however, McGavran discovered that wherever Christianity is expanding, one principle is always substantially behind it. Contrary to Protestant folk wisdom, the faith does not spread mainly through mass evangelism or media evangelism; it spreads mainly along the *social networks* of living Christians, especially to the social connections of transformed Christians and new Christians. The kinship and friendship networks of Christians provide "the bridges of God."[18] Though multiple causes synergize to produce growth, it is people who reach and bring people, much more than preaching, literature, campaigns, or anything else.[19]

Which types of social networks are the most prolific can vary from one context to another. McGavran observed that, in traditional, tribal, and agrarian societies, kinship networks are the most prolific; Christians in those churches mainly reach people to whom they are related by blood or marriage. In more urban and cosmopolitan societies, however, friendship networks are the most prolific; Christians in those churches mainly reach their friends, colleagues, and neighbors. McGavran also learned that God usually uses several relational bridges, not just one person, to reach most people. This is reminiscent of the reality reflected in 1 Corinthians 3:6, "I planted, Apollos watered, but God gave the growth." Some church growth blends the two patterns. Pastoral, neighborhood, or friendship contacts may reach one person in a pre-Christian family who then helps reach other family members.

Don Miller and Tetsunao Yamamori's significant study of world Pentecostal Christianity ratifies and extends these insights. Whereas Pentecostal churches in, for example, Latin America or sub-Saharan Africa often feature public crusades, such events are more effective in supporting the identity and unity of Christians than in reaching nonbelieving people. (Sometimes, crusades influence people in one church to join another church, and a crusade may raise the faith's public visibility.) The basis of virtually all conversions, however, is personal relationships between Christians and pre-Christian people. Typically, the mother of a family is reached first, followed by her children, and then the father. Following conversion, nurture and maturation in the faith are also mediated relationally. Indeed, people often experience their Pentecostal church like their new extended family; and in their small group life, they care for and minister to one another.[20]

McGavran's most counterintuitive discovery revealed that *new Christians* can be more reproductive than most church leaders assume. As a group, they are more reproductive than first-generation converts who have been Christians for many years; furthermore, they are especially more reproductive than people raised in the church—*if* the church appropriately deploys them in outreach.[21] This is the case for several reasons:[22]

- New Christians usually have many more contacts with pre-Christian people than do longtime church members.

- New Christians recall what it was like to try to make sense of their lives without Jesus Christ as Lord. Many longtime members have forgotten, and many people raised in churches never knew.

- New Christians still have about them the contagion of a new discovery, and the people in their social network who knew them "before Christ" are often attracted to the faith that can change people.

- Moreover, new Christians have not yet had the time to become linguistically corrupted by the "foreign languages" of preachers and theologians; they still understand and communicate in the target population's vernacular language.

McGavran's insight about the "bridges of God" is, almost undoubtedly, the most important strategic principle behind informed evangelism today. Whereas it substantially *describes* how effective outreach takes place (when it takes place), when churches *prescribe* and teach relational evangelism to their people, the principle's power is then amplified. At least one hundred million people across the earth are now Christians in part because churches and missions have consciously cooperated with this principle.[23]

Churches usually express the principle programmatically in their own way. A church may make a mailing list of every pre-Christian person in a new convert's social network and send those people engraved invitations to the service when the convert will join the church, with a reception to follow. Another church may list every convert's unchurched connections and then, with the convert, visit those persons, get in conversation with them, assess their receptivity, and invite them to become involved. Another church, when it receives new Christians into its ranks, may invite their "bridges" to stand with them as they are received; in time, the church's people come to assume that such evangelism is "normal Christianity"! An increasing number of churches take a redundant approach to cooperating with the principle. They may do some version of everything in this paragraph, and more.

◆   ◆   ◆   ◆

Once, in a conversation with McGavran, we identified some of the principle's "unfinished business." I suggested, "We know that people reach people in their social networks, but do we know *what kind* of Christians help pre-Christian people find their way? We know that strong *feelings* are typically involved in Christian conversion; how do our people make their friends and relatives feel? When our people do reach out effectively, what kinds of things do they *say*? And what kinds of things do they *do?*" McGavran smiled broadly, agreed that such questions were strategically important and that, to his knowledge, we did not know the answers to those questions. He unilaterally deputized *me* to do the field research to discover the answers!

I did that research, twenty to thirty days a year, for the next six years, in a range of denominational traditions and in such nations as Mexico, Canada, England, Australia, New Zealand, South Korea, Malaysia, and Singapore, in addition to the United States.[24] I interviewed converts and asked them to describe the person(s) who reached them, how they made them feel, what they said that helped make a difference, and so on. Also, when I led field seminars and workshops, I asked people who fit the following description to join my lunch table: they believed that evangelism was important and ought to be done, but they were not doing it.

I always had a full table! I interviewed at least eighty such groups, and I thereby discovered *the greatest barrier to evangelism* in our churches. When I asked them *why* they were not doing evangelism, even though they believed in it, they usually said something like, "I'm not that sort of person." When I asked them to describe the kind of person who does evangelism—to give me the adjectives—adjectives like these surfaced most often: dogmatic, holier-than-thou, narrow-minded, self-righteous, pushy, aggressive, overbearing, judgmental, hypocritical, insensitive, and fanatical. More than 90 percent of the adjectives were negative; sometimes they added terms like "totalitarian" and "spiritual fascists"! Once I gathered such data, I at last understood why so many of our people inwardly resist serving as "ambassadors for Christ."

When, however, I asked first-generation Christians in interviews and seminars to describe the person(s) who most served as *their* bridge into faith, they gave me an astonishingly contrasting set of adjectives—such as loving, caring, informed, understanding, accepting, affirming, interested, concerned, encouraging, supporting, kind, and credible. Notice, there is virtually *no* overlap between the two lists! Our people's folk wisdom (or the idea planted by the evil one) has convinced them that, to do evangelism, you have to become someone you wouldn't want to be, someone who you wouldn't even *want* to want to be. Occasionally, a seminar participant would nail the contrast as follows: "We have been duped into assuming that you cannot be like Jesus if you want to reach people for Jesus!" Sometimes, when they perceived that the kind of people who help other people find faith and new life are *not* like the first list but like the second, they concluded, "Being an ambassador for Christ *really* means being who we are already at our best or who we would love to be!" When enough of our people discover *that*, they will realize that they may be the best-prepared generation in centuries to fulfill the Great Commission. If enough of us discover this, our churches will become unstoppable movements.

You may have already anticipated the other contrasts. When I asked my lunch confidantes, "How do the 'evangelistic-type' people make non-Christian people *feel?*" the following "feeling words" were typical: guilty, damned, anxious, inadequate, angry, trapped, pressured, turned off, uncomfortable, and hopeless. New Christians, however, associated feelings like the following with *their* spiritual friends and guides: they felt valued, wanted, accepted, affirmed, respected, important, loved, worthwhile, comfortable, and hopeful. People tend to believe their own data, so when attendees saw the contrast between how effective evangelizers allegedly make people feel and how they actually make them feel, they often volunteered, "Well, I would *love* for my friends to feel like that!"

When I asked Christians what the "evangelistic-types" *say* and *do*, they gave many answers, but the most frequent were like these: they confront people, "invade their space," sling Bible texts at people, "preach at" people, and "push" people "to make a decision now." Their message is often an oversimplified single theme from the gospel, often about "getting born again" or "going to heaven."

What effective evangelizers *actually do and say* is the subject of the final section.

Conversations

Traditional evangelism is "presentation" evangelism; our most entrenched paradigm has programmed us to "present the gospel" to people. For at least a century, several generations of evangelical Protestants had been scripted to learn and rehearse a summary of the gospel and then orally present it to people in perhaps two minutes. We called it "personal evangelism." Along with "public evangelism" (such as revivals and crusades), these two approaches were the two tributaries of the Presentation River; presenting the gospel was *the* way to evangelize—to one person or to ten thousand. So we learned the Roman Road, and "evangelism explosion," and the four spiritual laws, while Latin American Christians rehearsed the "new life for all" formula. The content shifted some over time, but the basic approach did not. We would talk; they would listen; and then we would invite them to decide to believe the message and pray the prescribed "sinners prayer." If they did, we declared them "Christians"!

Most of us learned that we must do evangelism *that way*; the presentation paradigm was the only game plan in town. The paradigm did, indeed, fit the personality and strengths of a small minority of Christians, and through them the approach often produced some new Christians; but the paradigm did *not* fit the personality and strengths of most Christians. Consequently, most Christians who believed that evangelism should be done that way did not do it. Many people felt guilty throughout their entire Christian lives for their "failure" to do this.

Although Christians, indeed, can fail to do the will of God, the model exacerbated the problem. Most of our people have been unable to deliver "personal evangelism" because the model was insufficient for at least four reasons:[25]

- The formula we rehearsed typically left out too much of the gospel. Yes, the gospel *is* about second birth and eternal life, but it is also about the love, grace, righteousness, goodness, peace, and kingdom of God. It is also about the forgiveness of sins and freedom from sin; reconciliation and redemption; and justification, abundant life, sanctification, and more. Furthermore, the gospel includes Jesus' own message that calls us to a new life, this side of death, in which we live no longer for our own will but his; and his message's wider themes proclaim a vision of justice, peace, and a redeemed creation. So our traditional message often omitted much of the Message! Furthermore, our gospel summary sometimes refracted a theme that *did* get included. While, for instance, Christianity *is* partly about sharing by faith in Jesus' resurrection, it is even more about *fitting* us for heaven than it is about merely getting us to heaven.[26]

- When we presented a single theme of the gospel as though it were the whole gospel, we often observed two outcomes. First, if our single theme did not "scratch where they itched," or if our answer did not engage any question they were asking, they often inferred that Christianity was "irrelevant" to their questions, issues, and struggles. Second, if they did accept the one truth claim that we presented, they often assumed that was all Christianity was about. If we told them later that following Christ involves faithfulness in marriage, loving our enemies, working for peace, and sharing the faith, that wasn't clear in their original contract. They suspected a bait and switch.

- The presentation approach was based on an overly simplistic model of the communication of Christianity's message: a source, speaking perhaps a hundred words in two minutes, should be able to pour enough gospel content into the receiver's mind, without serious loss or distortion, to achieve "instant evangelism." The approach assumed that the receiver already had enough of a Christian background to understand Christianity's key terms, which, in our increasingly secular society, is less and less a valid assumption. The approach ignored the many other known factors involved in communication—that meaning gets communicated in many ways, from the credibility of the witness and the community to the role of liturgy, music, testimony, narrative, drama, poetry, visual symbols, the arts, the sacraments, and the receiver's own internal processing of ideas. As we suggested above, love communicates volumes. The presentation approach was also oblivious to the fact that, for most people, the process that leads to conversion takes weeks, months, or years—typically a season or two.

- The receivers often experienced what we called "personal evangelism" as *impersonal* salesmanship, propaganda, or institutional membership recruitment—too much like what they once experienced from a used-car salesman, a political candidate, or a fund drive. Indeed, the impersonal "hypodermic" approach to evangelism, in which we give people a "gospel shot" and hope it "takes," is often counterproductive. When they sense that the witnessing Christian does not even know them or understand them, or want to, the effort can confuse or alienate them. Sociologist Russell Hale once interviewed unchurched people in the eight most unchurched counties in the United States. He reported, "Most people can't hear until they have been heard."[27]

Russell Hale's 1979 project prepared us for the bad news and the good news that thirty years later have become even more blatant. The bad news is that the population that is even open to a one-way religious presentation is a declining market. The good news is that more people are interested in honest *two-way conversation* than ever before.[28] The ministry of conversation is the reproductive approach whose time has come.

Peter Berger, the sociologist, framed the informed understanding of conversion in societies such as ours. His research taught him that broadly there are three essential steps involved in someone's conversion. (1) Everyone has already been socialized into some worldview—a way of perceiving reality. (2) In a pluralistic society, in which there is more than one worldview, like Western society today, the main catalyst that opens people toward another worldview is *conversation* with someone who sees the world and lives life through a different worldview. (3) The process of conversion is complete when a person has been resocialized into the community that lives by the alternative worldview. So conversion takes place substantially through conversation, and not usually without it.[29]

Effectiveness in such conversation involves *skills* that, alas, some people have acquired in their socialization and others have not; fortunately, the skills can be taught and learned. A quarter century ago, many people became more effective conversationalists by studying Barbara Walters's *How to Talk with Practically Anybody about Practically Anything*.[30] More recently, four authors have reflected from their research in organizations and produced *Crucial Conversations: Tools for Talking When Stakes Are High*.[31] Although the book is written especially for people in business, education, and other organizations, the insights are astonishingly relevant to evangelistic conversation. We are already fully aware that conversation with people about, for example, getting a second chance, or making sense of their life, or experiencing their purpose in life through becoming a Christ-follower is, to say the least, a "crucial conversation." Our awareness is ratified in the authors' definition that qualifies a conversation as crucial: "A discussion between two or more people where stakes are high, opinions vary, and emotions run strong."[32] The authors teach a range of rather specific conversational skills, including skills for staying focused in the conversation (chapter 3), for making conversation *safe* (chapters 4 and 5), for listening with empathy (chapter 8), and for "speaking persuasively, not abrasively" (chapter 7).[33]

◆　　◆　　◆　　◆

The field with the clumsy name of "symbolic interactionism" provides perspectives for evangelizers—whether or not its founder, George Herbert Mead, had that in mind![34] For instance, Mead pioneered the idea that we tend to define our identity in ways that reflect how we believe "significant others" have defined us. ("Mead Lite," pop psychology's simplification, says, "I am not who I think I am. I am not who you think I am. I am who I think you think I am.") Evangelism, therefore, would involve knowing some pre-Christian people well enough, and living credibly enough, that when, in conversation, we told people who they could become as followers of Jesus, they would experience this as affirmation and revelation.

Again, Mead took very seriously the idea that within each of us an "internal conversation" takes place—many times, every day; we talk to ourselves much of the time. Moreover, we usually end up doing what we talk ourselves into doing. Then we tend to define ourselves as persons who do such things, for whom such things are important. This is a significant insight because, when people become new Christians, it is partly because they talked themselves into becoming Christians. In conversational evangelism, it is often useful to ask seekers what they say to themselves, what they tell themselves about themselves. If they say, for instance, "I'm a loser," we can often earn the permission to tell them they are "wrong" and to suggest what we believe God wants them to tell themselves and to suggest who they were created to be and, by the grace through Christ, can be. In my interviews with converts in recent years, I have asked, "How did you start talking to yourself differently in the season when you became a new Christian?" I discovered that new Christians can always get in touch with how they used to talk to themselves, how their self-talk started to change, and how their new self-talk helped change them.[35] We can often function as Christ's agents in coaching people on what to say to themselves. Furthermore, if what we do precedes or reinforces our self-definition to some degree, it is important to involve seekers and new believers in Scripture, prayer, group life, worship, service, witness, social involvement, and the other things Christians do *before* they define themselves as people of Christian faith.

In at least several ways, the ministry of conversation transcends the inherited presentation model. Conversations can represent more themes of the gospel than presentations can. The interchange in conversations, in which the other person tells us what they heard us say, gives us the chance to say it differently and to clarify our meaning. In conversation, we are still free to draw from a distilled version of the message we once learned. For example, I often share from the affirmations in the new life for all movement in Latin America:[36]

- God created all people for life.

- In their sin, people have forfeited much of what life was meant to be.

- God came in Christ to offer new life.

- We can accept and experience that new life through trusting and following Christ.

- If we become Christ-followers, we are called to be faithful to that new life in all of our relationships.

The new life for all summary is useful in part because (a) it engages people's increasing interest in experiencing real life *this* side of the grave; (b) it begins where Scripture does—with Creation rather than the Fall; and (c) it makes clear, and invites, the commitment to living our lives by God's will. In conversation, of course, we are liberated from parroting the message; it simply informs part of our contribution to the conversation. The other person typically experiences real conversation as *more personal* than what we have long called "personal evangelism." Finally, in real conversation there will usually be natural moments to include the Holy Spirit in the conversation. (We usually call that "prayer"!) Indeed, people sometimes sense the presence of God during the conversation, and even more often they perceive the presence as they see the conversation through a rearview mirror.

The ministry of conversation is not a modern, or postmodern, discovery. It is extensively modeled and reflected in the New Testament, and conversation across social networks substantially accounts for a majority of the converts in most Christian movements in most cultures and in most eras. Historians consistently credit preaching more than is warranted, and conversation (of clergy and especially laity) less than warranted. Whereas church history remembers "the great evangelists" as public *preachers* (perhaps because most writers of church history are ordained!), many of them, such as Jonathan Edwards, Charles G. Finney, and John Wesley, were also known in their lifetime as engaging conversationalists. Samuel Johnson reflected, "I hate to meet John Wesley; the dog enchants you with his conversation, and then breaks away to go and visit some old woman."[37]

John Wesley's *Journal* reports an extensive ministry of conversation, including letter writing. Wesley coached his people to visit with people in their homes and other places. Wesley taught that conversation permits us to discern what gospel themes people are most open to, and it is the way to "get within" people and to "suit all our discourse to their several conditions and tempers." He concluded that conversation is *necessary* to reach most people. "For, after all our preaching, many of our people are almost as ignorant as if they had never heard the gospel. . . . I have found by experience, that one of these has learned more from one hour's close discourse, than from ten years' public preaching."[38]

When Christians respond today to the unprecedented opportunity for conversation ministry, they typically experience four discoveries.

- When, in conversation with us, seekers are free to ask *questions* about the issues or doubts that have impeded their quest for faith and life, they are often verbalizing this to another person for the first time in their lives. When they ask the question, state the doubt, or "name the demon," that gets it out into the open, and it often begins to *lose* some of its immobilizing *power* over the person before his or her Christian conversation partner ever says much.

- Christians discover that their time spent studying Scripture and theology; rehearsing the gospel in liturgy; and reflecting upon sermons, lessons, and spiritual experience has *not* been a total waste as far as apostolic ministry is concerned! Indeed, Christians often discover that in those experiences they have been *prepared with* some of the insights and *answers* the seeker needs to hear. (Actually, God often gives us "beginner's luck"!)

- While Christians discover that their Christian formation has already given them some answers to the questions that seekers really do ask, they also discover that they do *not* have answers to some of the other questions that seekers ask. This discovery drives them back to Scripture, theology, and caucusing with other Christians who are engaged in witness and, from the questions that they could not at first answer, they *learn* more *useful theology* than they would learn in an entire degree program in "desk theology." Indeed, experience in apostolic ministry drives us to a deeper understanding of the gospel than time spent in church and academy, alone, could ever provide.[39]

- Finally, Christians discover that people ask some questions for which we do not have, and cannot find, fully satisfying answers. (Questions around suffering and natural evil are typical.) But Christians discover that is OK. Seekers do not need *all* of their questions answered; they only need *some* of their questions answered—enough to know that Christianity has some good reasons on its side. In any case, seekers do not usually expect Christians to have all of the answers to life's persistent questions. What helps them is not our answers to the questions we could not answer but rather the answers to those questions we could answer. What helps them most is not usually our answers; years later, they may recall almost nothing that we said. Most pre-Christian people, after all, have never had the opportunity to be in conversation with a trusted Christian who cared, listened, understood or wanted to understand, and wasn't defensive or judgmental in the face of doubts and questions. What makes the most difference is *the sacramental power of the ministry of conversation*.

◆　　◆　　◆　　◆

Case: Quest Community Church, Lexington, Kentucky

An increasing number of growing churches are discovering the imperative and subtle power of the ministry of conversation. One case will dramatize the point.

Quest Community Church in Lexington, Kentucky, averaged 148 people in attendance its first year. In its third year, Quest averaged 382; in its sixth year, 1,025. Now nine years old (as this is written), Quest ranks among the 50 fastest growing churches in the United States. It now averages more than 3,400 in weekend attendance and another 1,000 for Wednesday evening worship and teaching for believers. The church's total weekly attendance exceeds its (3,400) membership. The church is building a new auditorium, which will almost triple the seating capacity to 2,500. By the end of its seventh year, over 1,300 people had become new Christians at Quest. Then, in the church's eighth year, 1,200 people publicly accepted Christ; and in the ninth year 1,200 had committed through September.[40]

To reflect from this chapter's earlier themes, Quest Church's outreach is community based, nurtured, and encouraged; the whole church seems to function as the evangelism committee. Invitation typically takes place across the members' social networks; more than 80 percent of Quest's new Christians responded to one or more friends. But Quest Community Church was conceived from the ministry of conversation, and the church is rather obsessional about the leaders being in conversation with one another and with the members, and with members being in conversation with one another, and especially with the leaders and members being in conversation with pre-Christian people and seekers—within and beyond the church.

Pete Hise, the founding pastor and now the lead pastor, worked his way through Asbury Theological Seminary by waiting tables at a restaurant where he engaged in conversation with fellow waiters and patrons; at least ten became converts. When Pete graduated from divinity school, he served for several years as evangelism pastor at First Alliance Church in Lexington, Kentucky. Then, in 1999, about seventy First Alliance members joined him in planting the new church. From the beginning, Quest targeted unchurched people, including "people who don't like church" and people who had been "burned by church."

Quest church has been driven by what I call an apostolic agenda from its beginning. The church declares that its essential mission is "transforming unconvinced people into wholehearted followers of Jesus." The church understands itself to be "sent out" into the community and the world for this purpose. Hise looks upon Lexington as a mission field. He believes that our society is now so secular, and that secular people are so far from the life of faith, that there are no longer any Church Growth tips or techniques that a stagnant church can adopt and thereby use to grow; nor is it possible for a traditional church to merely *add* evangelism to everything else it is doing and see much difference. Pete says, "It's got to be the main thing." Sharon Clements, Quest's worship and arts pastor, adds that the church "has to love lost people. Without love, you will do more damage than good."

Quest Church embodies the key features of the apostolic congregation's worldwide profile. For instance:

- The church has proliferated congregations—four per weekend, as well as a believers' congregation on Wednesday nights, a recovery congregation on Friday nights, and a second campus in Frankfort, Kentucky.

- The church has targeted pre-Christian people who aren't at all like "good church people"; many have complex personal issues. The miracles that are now apparent in some of their lives have catalyzed responsiveness in many other people.

- Quest Church has virtually reinvented cultural relevance to the point of the complete "casualization of Christianity"! Quest has *no* dress code; the drink holders attached to each seat are for coffee mugs. Worship experiences feature the music, style, films, and humor of younger unchurched adults. One especially notices the use of indigenous expression: no King James verbiage, no hymnals, no choir (but, instead, singing ensembles). The sanctuary is now an "auditorium"; the testimonies are now people's "stories"; the foyer is the "atrium"; the ushers are "the receiving team." The church's auditorium features no traditional visual symbols of the faith, such as stained glass windows or even a cross.[41]

- The church is passionate about emotional relevance. Quest targets, welcomes, and engages people with issues, like addictions and compulsions, spiritual doubts and confusion, self-esteem and identity crises, debts and depression. Many visitors say they respond to the energy, the passion, the hope, and the extravagant love they experience there. Many converts report a new emotional freedom.

- Almost half of Quest's people are involved in LifeGroups, in which twenty to thirty people meet for teaching, ministry with one another, and (in smaller subgroups) for conversation and prayer. Since authentic community is one of the church's core values, they invite everyone to discover, through a LifeGroup, "friends who will do life with you."

- Quest features a range of outreach ministries to distinct populations—such as a thirteen-week support group experience for people experiencing separation or divorce, a Friday evening ministry for people with addictions who are in recovery, and "Good $ense" ministries of workshops and counseling for people with financial struggles.

- The church is substantially involved in the world mission of its tradition, the Christian and Missionary Alliance, which is one of the three strongest mission denominations in the United States (considering its ratio of members to the number of supported overseas missionaries). Quest sends out multiple short-term mission teams per year and supports mission on several continents.

Quest Community Church, however, is not merely a clone of the generic apostolic congregation profile. The church has developed its own ways of engaging a city. Take Questapalooza, for example—"a party for the city." The church now schedules this one-day music and arts festival each fall. The back windows of church members' cars become a thousand or more "moving billboards" announcing the festival. The event gives every member an "excuse" to invite their friends for the weekend's program featuring fireworks; carnival rides; and noted Christian rock bands, singing groups, and soloists. The church, during the festival, publicly baptizes a roster of new believers while each tells his or her story on videotape. Going *this* public with their commitment has deep meaning for the converts, and the experience attracts new people toward the church and the faith. More than 1,800 people came to the first Questapalooza; more than 6,500 came to the third.

Most of all, however, Quest Community Church is about the ministry of conversation. The church was conceived in conversations at a restaurant. The favored mode of Christian witness is faithful conversation. The LifeGroup meetings split for a time into smaller groups for conversation. Quest Church modified the Friday experiences for the recovery community to include a time for conversation every Friday night.

Quest Church's greatest innovation can be observed at the conclusion of almost every worship experience. The form of the evangelistic invitation is to come forward and get into conversation with someone who will help the person, who is now seeking, to process the Christian possibility for his or her life; the seeker's conversation partner will listen and talk as long as necessary. *All* of Quest's several hundred leaders, and many other members, are committed, trained, and available for this ministry. They report profound meaning in "midwifing" new life.

The leaders reflect together on their experiences in evangelical conversation so that they may improve in the ministry. They discovered that the conversations are more often about life, and how to live one's life, than about doctrine or ideology. Sharon Clements reports, "Often, the single most important thing we do in these conversations is ask questions, and then listen." Quest's leaders have learned that it is important to take enough time to earn the right to be heard. With the population Quest reaches, this ministry requires not being judgmental toward the other person; and it may involve appropriate self-disclosure such as, "I once had that same doubt." Quest's people have learned to listen for feelings as well as meanings, and then to rephrase what they are hearing so that the seekers sense and feel that their conversation partner understands them and empathizes with them.

Sharon Clements reports that, often, "People are moved when you give them time." She reports that leaders often experience a lengthy conversation following a service as "an inconvenience"; lunch, a meeting, another service, or something is usually scheduled and waiting. "But our people take the inconvenience of evangelism as a joy." Pete Hise believes that to reach pre-Christian people today, a church "*must* create a culture of authentic conversation."

CHAPTER SIX

EVANGELIZING PRE-CHRISTIAN PEOPLE: A NARRATIVE PERSPECTIVE

How do pre-Christian people, who do not even know what we Christians are talking about, become Christ-followers? I have been asking questions like that for almost five decades.

As I mentioned in the preface, I was raised fairly secular in Miami, Florida, although somehow I knew the Lord's Prayer, and anyone in my family could tell you the name of the church we stayed away from! In 1955, at the age of seventeen, I experienced a religious awakening. I visited several churches. The Fulford Methodist Church welcomed me and "adopted" me before I had believed or experienced much at all. Within months, I discovered the gift of faith; I was given new lenses through which to view my life and the world; and I experienced profound life change. Within several more months, my mom and dad and several friends were also Christians.

In the summer of 1962, while I was still in divinity school, I spent the summer in ministry to the people of Muscle Beach in California. They were a smorgasbord of humanity—the muscle crowd, beatniks, homosexuals, surfers, sunbathers, addicts, gamblers, and others. They were different populations sharing the same beach, with little interaction between groups. As far as I was concerned, however, almost all of those people had one thing in common. They had no idea what I was talking about! They had no Christian memory, no church to return to. They were secular people in the sense that they had never been substantially influenced by the Christian religion in any viable form. They were even more secular than I had been while growing up in Miami. Most of them did not know the Lord's Prayer, and they could *not* tell me the name of the church they stayed away from. Many did not know the name of the church their parents or grandparents had stayed away from, though they *all* had heard that churches were "boring" and "irrelevant" places!

I found myself identifying with secular people, believing that they mattered to God more than they knew (and more than most churches knew), and I believed that churches should, and could, reach them. I became obsessed with the challenge of communicating the meaning of Christianity's message to "pagans." To make as much sense of this challenge as I could, I did a PhD in communication studies at Northwestern University. Over the years, I interviewed several thousand secular people and more than one thousand converts out of secularity. I studied and interviewed Christian advocates to secular people on three continents.[1] I studied churches that reach secular people.[2] I studied how these churches do ministry with people who do not yet believe.[3] Over the decades, I have learned some things worth sharing.

How Protestant Folk Wisdom Views Evangelism

The question of *how* to reach pre-Christian people has not escaped the interest of other church leaders, of course, and over the years I have learned what many other leaders believe on this matter. My research has confirmed four claims that are already prominent in Protestant folk wisdom: (1) We have to *believe* the gospel. (2) We have to be people of *prayer*. (3) We have to *obey* the will of God (including the Great Commission). (4) We have to *love* lost people. So most Christian leaders already know that faith, prayer, obedience, and love are indispensable. If Samuel Johnson was right, however, that "people need to be reminded more often than they need to be instructed," we need to be reminded of these commonplace insights often.

The four insights are essential, but they are not enough; if they were enough, we would already be gathering harvests in most places, worldwide. Sometimes the apostolic cause is advanced when we embellish one of the basic insights and help people rediscover it, as if for the first time. For instance, while reminding us of the gospel's importance, Leander Keck contended, "The gospel is the only thing we have to offer the world that it doesn't already have."

My research has *dis*confirmed three beliefs that are widely held in Protestant Christianity:

- The most widespread approach to outreach that churches often have in mind involves two phases. In the first phase, the church will become more "renewed" (or "revitalized" or "healthy"); *then*, in phase two, the church will reach out to unchurched people. The problem is they do not get around to phase two. They never feel renewed, revitalized, or healthy enough to get into mission.

- The second disconfirmed belief assumes that when (and *if*) we do get around to evangelizing, we will do it by "preaching" at people, or by a monologue presentation of some kind. (I have suggested that two-way conversation *with* people is far more reproductive than preaching or witnessing *at* people.)

- The third widely held belief contrasts with the second: some church leaders claim that we need not witness at all. We only need to establish a caring *presence* among people; if we let our "light shine before men," that is enough. Actually, being present with people is always necessary, but it is almost never enough.

"As Simple as Possible"

Since much of what we think we know has been disconfirmed, one question cannot be escaped: *Why*, on the matter of a church's main business, are Christian leaders wrong about as often as they are right? The most cogent explanation that I have found can be framed within the statements of two twentieth-century scientists.

1. Arthur Eddington taught astronomy and astrophysics at Cambridge University, while reading much more widely. His *Relativity Explained* interpreted and advanced Albert Einstein's theory of relativity to a much wider, educated public. (Eddington was also a devout Quaker Christian who published *Why I Believe in God* in 1930.) From Eddington's astonishingly broad knowledge, he was known for this declaration: "Not only is the universe more [complex] than we imagine; it is more [complex] than we *can* imagine."[4]

The experiences of Christian intellectuals consistently validate this insight. When, for example, we first study theology, we discover that the doctrine of the Triune God, the message of the kingdom of God, the doctrine of grace, and the process of Scripture's canonization are much more complex than we once imagined. Likewise, reaching a pre-Christian population represents a complex challenge; if they speak another tongue or are illiterate, that compounds the complexity. In the graduate program in which I teach, every PhD student at the dissertation stage discovers that the topic she or he decided to research is enormously more complex than she or he ever imagined!

The fact of complexity does not mean that reaching *some* informed understanding is impossible; but the quest for knowledge only rewards the persistent student, and the quest for new knowledge only rewards the persistent researcher. Once one really understands something, one can eventually explain one's new understanding, and rather simply, but that relative simplicity is reached by (and not without) working through the complexity.[5]

2. The other statement is from Einstein: "Everything should be made as simple as possible, but not simpler." That statement, with surgical precision, exposes the church's two biggest problems in regard to the knowledge that informs our theological understanding, our ministry, and our witness.

First, many leaders in the church's academy do not make their knowledge "as simple as possible." They often bury their insights in verbal obscurity; people educated in their field *may* understand their technical language, but people who are not so educated "don't have a prayer." Their discoveries *could* make a difference, but the insights are not sufficiently available to church leaders and thoughtful Christians. (C. S. Lewis, by comparison, was not the twentieth century's greatest theologian, but he has had the greatest enduring influence; he made Christian truth "as simple as possible" in clear, imaginative prose, including fiction.) In every generation, the challenge facing all academic leaders in the church's service is to pay the price to understand a complex topic AND then to make truth "as simple as possible."

Second, the prevailing tendency of church leaders (and political leaders, and leaders in other sectors) is to make it "simpler" than is possible, while at the same time *denying* the complexity. In peer group conversation, and usually over time, the group socially constructs a folk wisdom that shapes the church or mission's perceptions, priorities, policies, and programs, and the folk wisdom is usually much "simpler" than is "possible" without some sacrifice of truth. Some obvious examples would include the following: a good sermon will feature three points and a poem; 11:00 a.m. is always the best time to worship God; a daily devotional forms devout Christians. Likewise, if we want to reach people, we will let our light shine, we will present to people the statements in a pamphlet, or we will experience church renewal first. Folk wisdom comes from a people's reflection and conversation upon their shared experiences, and sometimes its expressions through maxims, slogans, or stories helps the people make some sense within their complex challenge. But folk wisdom is often (perhaps usually) insufficient, and it almost always pales in comparison to the "as simple as possible" made available through the best scholarship—and not without it.

◆   ◆   ◆   ◆

In chapter 2, we profiled the apostolic congregations across the earth that reach pre-Christian populations. Based upon many field studies from many scholars, the profile attempts to describe effective apostolic congregations as simply as possible.

In chapter 5 and in this chapter, we now ask *how* effective apostolic congregations go about reaching people. Once again, many church leaders will assume from their tradition or their peer group that they already know the answer: they will often attribute the church's magnetism to the contemporary music, the celebrative spirit, the preaching, the band, the drama, the testimony, the way they welcome guests, or some other feature of the apostolic congregation's public worship services. Although their approach to worship does, indeed, contribute to their appeal, and does help communicate and dramatize the message and its meanings, and is undeniably a major "front door" factor in reaching the community, few apostolic congregations count totally (or even primarily) on worship services to reach people. I have already introduced the role of many "side doors"—such as small groups, lay ministries, and outreach ministries—that advance the church's local mission, as well as the indispensable roles of community, compassion, connections, and conversations in effective evangelism (see chapter 5).

This chapter continues the move to the "as simple as possible" that becomes available when we reflect upon research and experience for long enough. We now identify some outreach dynamics that take place below the surface, which observers seldom notice, which often escape the notice of a church's leaders,[6] and which typically account even more for the conversion growth of apostolic congregations. What below-the-radar outreach dynamics is it now possible to identify? To frame our question a slightly different way: *How* do people with no Christian memory, who are not like "good church people," experience faith and new life? Some of the answers to this question are reflected in the earliest case study that is available to us.

The Earliest Case Study

In Bethlehem and the southern kingdom of Judah, some 1,100 years before Christ, an extended drought devastated the region. It was a time of famine. Crops were withering on the stalks and vines; sheep were dying on the hills. One day, Naomi's family realized that they could not continue to live in Bethlehem. They decided to join a colony of Jews who had migrated to a farming region of Moab where the rains still fell and the soil was lush. So Naomi, her husband, and their two sons moved to Moab. Their destination was only 50 miles or so to the east, on the other side of the Jordan River and the Dead Sea; but they were entering a very different cultural world. The Moabites spoke another language; they lived by different values, beliefs, and customs; and they worshiped a high god named Chemosh, who the Jews believed was not worthy of human devotion.

Sometime following their move, Naomi's husband died. Later, her two sons met and married Moabite young women, and they brought their "pagan" wives into Naomi's now extended household. Then Naomi's two sons both died. By now the rains had returned to Judah and all of Naomi's reasons for the move to Moab were history. So she announced to her two daughters-in-law that she would return to her home and to her people. The two young women walked with her as far as the Jordan River.

Naomi then turned to them and advised them to return to Moab, to their people. One daughter-in-law reluctantly complied, but the other young woman, Ruth, responded, "Do not press me to leave you or to turn back from following you! For where you go, I will go; Where you lodge, I will lodge; your people shall be my people, and your God my God."

Naomi returned to Bethlehem with Ruth in her company. Now Ruth had to cope as the foreigner in another culture, but Naomi coached Ruth in the ways of the Hebrew people. In time, Ruth met and married Naomi's cousin Boaz. Later, Ruth gave birth to a son, Obed. The book of Ruth leaves us with the impression that they lived "happily ever after."

"Your God, my God." The biblical story of Ruth may be the earliest available case of religious conversion from some other religious worldview to devoted faith in Israel's Yahweh. Why did Ruth turn to Naomi's God and now share Naomi's faith? The available answers are important because, in general, they reveal some of the typical reasons almost *anyone* adopts the fulfillment of the faith of Abraham in Jesus Christ. Notice that Ruth became a convert 600 years before a messiah was explicitly promised; 1,100 years before his birth; and 3,000 years before Billy Graham or billboards and bumper stickers, tracts and pamphlets, radio and television evangelists, and all the other things that many church leaders assume are necessary to reach people. What might we learn from this ancient case study? Let's reflect on ten insights that can at least be inferred from the case of Ruth.[7]

◆　　　◆　　　◆　　　◆

1. Ruth's turning to Israel's God was a gradual *process* that took place over time. There is no hint of a one-time transformative event, no reason to believe this was a case of "instant evangelism." Although the process was probably punctuated by events, and by significant experiences that Ruth could later recall, it was essentially a process. For most people, conversion is analogous to the birth of a baby, which is a process, but which is also punctuated by events, such as conception, and the first time the mother notices the baby moving, and delivery. Although we know of rare possible exceptions, there are not many more instant conversions than there are instant babies!

2. Ruth's shift in religious allegiance from Chemosh to Yahweh occurred through a *chain of experiences* over time. Communication theorists partly explain attitude change and conversion by the cumulative effect of many communications and experiences over time. Willow Creek Community Church confirmed the theory and popularized the analogy of the chain of experiences. Each significant experience adds a link in the chain that leads to faith and new life.

This visual analogy is remarkably useful in reflecting about apostolic ministry. For instance, it suggests that every link in a chain is as important as every other link. If that is true, then the widespread assumption that the last link is the only link that matters is mistaken and counterproductive.[8] Every experience that mediates God's revelation really matters. The chain analogy encourages Christians who are better at providing a first link for people, or a middle link, than a last link. The analogy suggests an appropriate apostolic approach to people at specific moments: get to know them well enough to infer where they are in the process while asking the Holy Spirit to lead you in providing the next link. Willow Creek's people sometimes suggest that it takes perhaps eight conversations before someone steps over the line, but I think it is desirable to reflect upon all of the kinds of experiences that help people find their way. In my lengthy interviews with converts, they typically talk about thirty experiences (more or less) that moved them along.

Charles G. Finney's understanding of the four sources of such experiences helped me organize what converts reported.[9] First, Finney believed that God is orchestrating the chain of experiences to make it possible for the person to become a Christ-follower and, more specifically, some of the specific revelatory experiences come directly from God. My interviews confirmed this; the "God thing" that converts report most often is the experience of answered prayer—often several such experiences.

Second, Finney observed that the *word of God*, or specific Christian truth claims, or specific biblical texts exercise a kind of sovereign power in the seeker's soul; the person thinks about them over and over. My interviews confirmed this; converts are very articulate in stating a text or idea that would not let them go.

Third, Finney observed *Christians* playing an indispensable role in the conversion of others, especially through the ministry of Christian witness. My interviews confirmed and expanded this insight. Christians provide experiential links by befriending sinners, listening to them, identifying with them, praying for them, praying with them, believing in them, pulling for them, inviting them, and so on. Sometimes a Christian provides a link without knowing it—as when the seeker observes a Christian praying, or loving someone else, or living with integrity.

Fourth, Finney emphasized that *converts* are contributors to their own conversion much more than theologians have often understood; they do some things that advance the process. My interviews confirmed this too. Converts report doing some things, very intentionally, like going to church, attending a Bible study, reading a Christian book, asking questions, trying to pray, and even "trying Christianity on for size to see if it fits"; that is, they often start trying to live as (they think) Christians live, to see if the experiment is self-authenticating.

The chain of experiences is not a perfect analogy of the conversion process. In conversion, for instance, the "links" are not all the same size; that is, not all the experiences are equally significant. Again, in a way we cannot visualize by using the chain image, some experiences are essentially repeated. (For instance, virtually no one "gets" the message of justification by grace the first time they think about it. That message has to be reinforced many times before most people understand and believe it.) Furthermore, often the convert's progress is not smooth and continual; people may get stuck, or relapse, or drop out and come back later, or they may take a step or two backward before moving forward again. Nevertheless, Ruth's conversion (like most) was a process, with a chain of significant experiences that changed her self-understanding, her worldview, and her relationship with God over time.

3. Ruth's new possibility was mediated through *relationships* with people who already lived by the faith of Abraham. Her friendship with Naomi obviously comes to

mind. But her marriage with Chilion, Naomi's son, would have been another path of grace. In time, undoubtedly, other Hebrew people in the expatriate colony in Moab also befriended her.

Converts, today, typically cite several believers who served as their "bridges," which is reminiscent of Paul's observation in 1 Corinthians 3:6: "I planted, Apollos watered, but God gave the growth." Behavioral scientists today feature the role of significant others in all of our lives. Significant others are the people who become especially important to us, who often serve as role models; we usually see ourselves much as we think our significant others see us. And we usually believe, and see the world, much as they do.[10] (In relational evangelism, a few Christians becoming *that* trusted in the person's life is usually a prominent factor in the process.)

4. The *credibility* of Yahweh's believers in Moab would have energized Ruth's search. Helmut Thielicke, a German theologian and preacher in secular Germany, observed that the most important factor in whether or not secular people take the Christian message seriously is "the credibility of the witnesser" (and the credibility of the witnessing community). Secular people, he said, examine to see if we actually live in the house that we invite them to enter.[11]

For years, I checked Thielicke's thesis in interviews with secular people and converts, and I discovered that the credibility issue can cut one or more of three ways: (a) Some people wonder whether we really believe what we say we believe. (b) Some people assume we believe it, but they wonder whether we really live by what we believe. (c) Some people assume we believe it, and live by it; they wonder whether it makes much difference. They tend, therefore, to dismiss limited versions of Christianity that focus on the soul, the family, and church attendance but ignore matters like peace, justice, and the health of creation.

So we can infer that Ruth perceived in Naomi authentic qualities she had not noticed in Moabite women; the worship of Chemosh did not produce women like Naomi. Let's not overlook the credibility she saw in Chilion. If Moabite society was like most primal societies, even today, most Moabite men treated their wives as little more than pleasure-giving, childbearing animals. I imagine that Ruth found a meaning and equality in her marriage with Chilion that was unlike any Moabite marriage she had observed. Furthermore, she undoubtedly met many credible believers within the Jewish Diaspora.

5. Ruth experienced the Hebrew community *wanting* her, *understanding* her, *loving* her, and *believing* in her. Maybe, she thought, their God does too; the Moabites believed that Chemosh, their high god, was indifferent to his people. In Church Growth studies today, we have rediscovered that many people go where they are wanted most. They respond to communities that understand them, believe in them, and have goodwill toward them.

6. The Hebrew community helped Ruth acquire the essential *knowledge* of the faith of Abraham, and in time she knew that material by heart. So she knew the great story that began when Abraham demonstrated radical obedience. She knew the history and stories we find in Genesis through Joshua. She knew the Shema and all the psalms that had emerged in Hebrew life, including two psalms from the pen of Moses. These texts, stories, themes, and ideas now informed Ruth's internal conversation, day after day.

7. Ruth was, essentially, *adopted* into the Hebrew community. Before she believed or experienced anything, she was included in the expatriate Hebrews' fellowship and their worship, their rituals and their prayers, and she participated in their celebrative festivals, such as the Passover. To some degree, like most converts, she was socialized into the community's worldview; most of us, over time, believe what our primary community believes.[12] Like most postmodern converts to Christianity in the West today, she "belonged" before she "believed."[13]

8. Ruth engaged in many *conversations* that moved her along the conversion process. Converts today report that their understanding was helped some by teaching, preaching, and other presentations, but their conversations with believers—honest, open, two-way conversations—made much more of a difference. We are discovering the ministry of conversation. Peter Berger and Thomas Luckmann's *Social Construction of Reality* features three essential phases in *any* kind of worldview conversion: (a) Everyone has been socialized, from their early years, into a worldview—a way of seeing reality. (b) In a pluralistic society, with multiple worldviews, the mechanism that opens someone to an alternative worldview is *conversation* with someone who lives by the alternative worldview. (c) The process of worldview conversion is essentially completed when the convert has been resocialized into a community that lives by the alternative worldview.

Some 1,100 years before Christ, Ruth was in conversation with Naomi, Chilion, and other faithful Hebrews. She undoubtedly initiated many conversations, for she would have had many questions. Even more important, these experiences influenced her day-by-day internal conversation. People essentially talk themselves into living a different life.

9. Her conversion models two imperative perspectives on effective evangelism: (a) We begin *where people are*, rather than where we would like them to be. So we begin with whatever they already know or believe that we can build on. We begin with the questions they ask, the needs they reflect, and with the issues and struggles of their lives. (b) For most people, including Ruth, the faith is even *more "caught" than "taught."* So from the friendships, the significant others, the fellowship, the participation in Hebrew festivals and liturgical life, and from the many conversations (including her inner conversation) she gradually experienced the contagion of the faith of Abraham.

10. Ruth discerned before her conversion, and experienced with her conversion, that *turning to the true God makes an enormous difference in one's life.* She would have known that changing one's faith is not a decision made at the recreational level, like, "I used to cheer for the Packers, but now I cheer for the Bears." Changing one's faith goes much deeper and is much more serious because we become like the gods we worship and the convictions and values we live for. Ruth would have immediately detected the fraud in the eighteenth-century Enlightenment's teaching that, deep down, all religions are the same. She knew better from experience. Chemosh and Yahweh were not identical twins, and the two religions were not superficially different ways of understanding the same high God; they were profoundly different approaches to transcendence that led to very different kinds of life experiences.

Postscript

Most churches are usually not aware that the story of Ruth introduces perhaps a greater reason to evangelize. Most churches evangelize (*if* they evangelize) because of the "definite promises" of the gospel—such as the promise of heaven, or a second chance, or healthy self-esteem. Ruth's story reminds us of the gospel's "indefinite promise" that following Jesus as Lord leads to the most adventurous and meaningful life available to people in this world—an abundant life with many experiences that no one can forecast.

Let's resume Ruth's story. The book of Ruth leaves us with Ruth and Boaz meaningfully married, and with a son, Obed. The story continues. In time, Obed married and his wife gave birth to Jesse. Jesse grew up, married, and his wife gave birth to David. Please notice (if my math is still with me), twenty-three generations later, from the lineage of Ruth, Jesus of Nazareth was born in Bethlehem. Ruth stands as the Bible's greatest exemplar of the most extravagant indefinite promise—proclaimed by Isaiah and repeated in Paul's Corinthian correspondence: Our eyes have not seen, our ears have not heard, and our hearts have never imagined all that God has in mind for those who love the Lord.

In the ministry of evangelism, we are supremely privileged to invite and welcome people into the great adventure.

CHAPTER SEVEN

LEADING THE CHANGE FROM TRADITION TO MISSION

Most of the churches in North America and Europe *could* reach and serve many more people than they currently reach; a majority of churches could reach and serve more people than they even imagine; and many churches (at least one in five) could become local Christian movements. An all-too-common story, however, reveals why churches seldom fulfill their mission.

Most local churches, for perhaps their first fifteen years as a church, once reached new people, changed lives, and influenced the wider community; indeed, that first-generation church understood local mission to be their main business. Over time, however, caring for members took increasing precedence over reaching pre-Christian people, and the community changed while the church changed less, and so the church's membership strength leveled off for years fifteen through thirty-five.

Then, by the church's thirty-fifth birthday, the community had changed much more than the church. The church's approach was no longer indigenous to the community's culture, and the community's people now visited the church much less. The church felt like more and more of the community's people were living non-Christian lifestyles, and perceived some of the people as threats. So the church circled the wagons, and became absorbed in the liturgical year, and totally (perhaps unconsciously) redefined its main business as ministering to "our people" and perpetuating "our tradition."

Most second-generation (and older) churches in the United States perpetuate ways of "doing church" that they received from two periods in the past: (1) the century when their forebears in Europe crossed the Atlantic and brought their tradition to the New World, and (2) the 1950s and early 1960s, when mainline denominations last thrived, and grew, and felt they were making a difference. "Old East Side Church" has been going through the motions for longer than anyone who now attends there can remember.[1]

For a long time, Old East Side Church has been losing from 5 to 8 percent of its members per year as members drop out, transfer to other churches, or die. Meanwhile, Old East Side has received new members equivalent to perhaps 3 to 6 percent of its membership per year as some of the members' children join, as some people transfer from other churches, and as the very occasional "converts" join.[2] The math quickly demonstrates that Old East Side has experienced a 2 percent (more or less) net loss in most years for a long time. Small net losses add up. If a 500-member church experiences a net loss of only 2 percent per year, in ten years it has 408 members; in a quarter century it has 302 members.

Old East Side Church *does not feel* the crisis for many years, however, for two reasons. (1) For quite awhile, the church can receive more and more money from fewer and fewer people, so they can postpone the economic recession that *will* overwhelm the church some day. (2) They do receive *some* new members almost every year without changing. This seduces Old East Side's leaders into assuming that they can turn the decline around by trying a little harder or by making minor adjustments.

In 1965, Wallace Fisher's *From Tradition to Mission* advanced the case that his Lutheran tradition's problem was deeper than minor adjustments could address;[3] the solution, he believed, was no less (and no other) than a full recovery of Christianity's *mission* to the community and the world. This book stands, with some of my earlier writing,[4] in Fisher's lineage, and with several other movements and literatures.[5] Meanwhile, since 1965, an endless series of lesser visions for churches, such as becoming boomer churches, metachurches, vibrant churches, blended churches, avant-garde churches, user-friendly churches, innovative churches, healthy churches, organic churches, or emerging churches—and twenty or more other models, slogans, and wrinkles—have each triggered a season of interest, and occasional enthusiasm. But, in time, church leaders experienced them promising more than they delivered and they waited for the next bandwagon. I have come to believe, however, that every model except some version of the ancient and perennial apostolic model will fail to deliver on most of our reasonable hopes.

"There Is Nothing More Difficult to Take in Hand"

Many church leaders, of course, have discovered that *saying* "our church needs to change" and become more missional does not lead inevitably to *achieving* the desired changes! (In some cases, a church adopts the new missional jargon but *nothing* else seems to change!) Perceiving the need for strategic change is but the first step in a serious change effort.

The second step, for leaders of churches (and leaders of other kinds of organizations), is to face the brute fact that *leading change is difficult*. Serious students of human affairs have long known this. Almost 500 years ago, Machiavelli warned would-be change agents, "There is nothing more difficult to take in hand, more perilous to conduct, or more uncertain in its success, than to take the lead in the introduction of a new order of things." He featured this warning on the title page of *The Prince*, in the apparent hope that no reader would miss it.

Today, ideas like "People resist change" and "The only people who want change are wet babies" are common expressions of our folk wisdom. Like much of folk wisdom, such maxims are related to truth but are not precisely true. Psychologists suggest that what people usually resist is not change per se; they resist experiencing several psychological dynamics that attach to change.

When we know these dynamics, we can already infer some of what a change effort should involve: (1) People typically resist the *loss* of what they are already familiar with, that which used to work and may still work fairly well. They, therefore, need to understand and desire the *advantage* that the proposed change would bring. (2) People often have some anxiety about the *unknown*; so they need to *visualize* what the change would look like. (3) People typically resist loss of personal *choice*. They resist imposed change; so leaders need to *involve them* in the change effort if they are to "own" the changes that are proposed. (4) Many people with experience in organizations have lived long enough to see some bad, trendy, or half-baked change proposals come and go; so they need adequate *information* and *time* to consider the current change proposal.

Perspectives for Addressing Change

Spiritual Perspectives

No reader will be surprised to read that certain spiritual features are typically prominent in apostolic congregations and, therefore, these features should characterize churches that want to turn to a more apostolic agenda. My field research in growing churches with an apostolic orientation has especially observed five recurrent features.

- Many of their people seem to be deeply rooted, even immersed, in *Scripture*. These roots typically go much deeper than a daily Bible reading can take people. They know much of the biblical canon more or less by heart, and they see life and the world through the lenses of New Testament faith.

- Many of their people are disciplined and expectant in *prayer*. They pray for lost people who need to be found, and they pray to be led to lost people in whom the Holy Spirit is moving.

- Many of their people are deeply driven by compassionate *goodwill* for lost people—including really lost people—who are not at all like "good church people."

- They are consciously *obedient* to the will of God, especially the Great Commission to communicate the gospel and make new disciples among pre-Christian populations. This is not a reluctant obedience; they would rather do that than anything else.

- Whereas many of their people take advantage of much that their church offers in helping them become biblical, devoted, compassionate, and obedient, the people primarily take *responsibility* for their formation and for who they become in Christ.

Leaders who perceive that their churches do not yet have a sufficient critical mass of Christians who are biblical, devout, obedient, compassionate, and self-responsible can therefore easily identify some areas to focus change efforts. So much help is now available in the literatures of spiritual formation, Christian education, and church renewal that this chapter will not pretend to contribute very much, with the exception of two revolutionary ideas:

1. Churches typically make the mistake of waiting until "everybody is on board" before they feel as though they can cooperate with the true church's main business. They wait forever, or until they forget what they were waiting for. The reality of the matter is that a church's leaders will not need for all of their members, or even a majority, to fit that spiritual profile to get moving in local mission; indeed, while we yearn for *all* of our people to be devoted and empowered, something like 10 percent of a

church's on-board members will usually constitute a sufficient critical mass for experiencing much greater growth. Think about it. If just a tenth of one's membership is on board, and they average among them reaching only one new person per year, that represents 10 percent more growth per year than the church would have otherwise experienced.

2. Churches do not even need to wait until 10 percent of the membership is compassionate, obedient, and so on before they begin reaching out and inviting. If, for example, one or two Sunday school classes, or two or three small groups, or one of a church's three congregations, or even 2 percent of the membership is on board, you need not wait for the others. You can already reach some people, and a stream of new people entering the church's ranks, who have recently discovered grace and new life, will renew the tired old church and catalyze more depth and devotion than the church would ever experience by waiting to reach out until everyone was on board.

So there are no compelling reasons for waiting for everyone, rather than moving with the people who are already committed.

Organizational Perspectives

Some readers may be surprised to discover that, in addition to spiritual perspectives, there are also organizational perspectives for addressing change in churches. Many church leaders resist even thinking of their church as "an organization." It is fashionable to say, "The church is not an organization; it is an organism."

In *Leading and Managing a Growing Church*,[6] I suggested that such thinking is consistent with an ancient and heretical line of thought. The heresy was called Docetism, which was a branch of ancient Gnosticism. The Docetists believed that matter was evil, and the human body was especially evil, so it was unthinkable that the Son of God would actually take on human flesh. Consequently, they believed, Jesus was "fully God" but he was not really "fully human"; his body had the appearance of a human body but was not a real human body. The equivalent thinking today, in the doctrine of the church, maintains that while a church may look like an organization (with officers, facilities, plans, budgets, and so on), the body of Christ is *not really* a human organization.

Why is this connection important to point out? One reason is that this refusal to take the church seriously, as a human organization, undermines the futures of countless churches.

Let me suggest that a local church *is* an organization, though a unique kind of organization. In *Leading and Managing a Growing Church*, I unpacked that uniqueness as follows:

> The church is, or should be, different from McDonald's, Sears, Rotary, GM, IBM, MIT, and P&G. Ignoring the fact that each of those seven organizations is very different from the other six, five things (at least) do make the church a different kind of organization:

> (1) The church has a distinctive *source*. Christ built it, on the rock of faith in him as Messiah and risen Lord, to be the New Israel, the Body of Christ, and the extension of his incarnation.

(2) From the ancient apostles, the church has a distinct *message*—the gospel. That is why Leander Keck, former dean of Yale Divinity School, coaches church leaders to "spend your life offering the gospel to the world, because it is the only thing we have to offer the world that it doesn't already have."

(3) The church has a distinct *purpose*—to reach the peoples of the earth, to help them become reconciled to God, liberated from their sins, restored to God's purpose, and deployed in God's wider mission seeking health, peace, justice, and salvation for all people and (some would add) all creation.

(4) Through such sources as the Ten Commandments, the Sermon on the Mount, and the Great Commandment to love God and neighbor, the church is given the *ethic* that should limit, shape, and focus how Christians do Kingdom business.

(5) As "no one can say 'Jesus is Lord' except by the Holy Spirit" (1 Cor. 12:3), not much else that is supremely important in our total mission is likely to succeed without Third Person power behind, attending, and blessing our efforts.

Though the church is a different kind or organization, however, it is still an organization. In common with other organizations, the church is an interdependent aggregation of people with some shared history, identity, and culture, who pull together in coordinated activities to achieve the organization's objectives. Granting its distinctive source, message, mission, ethic, and *reliance*, churches nevertheless have much in common with other organizations, particularly other voluntary organizations. When churches achieve their objectives, many of the reasons are the same as when other kinds of organizations achieve their objectives.[7]

Four Theories for Informing Change

In the twentieth century, scholars learned more about organizations, leadership, management, organization development, and what makes some organizations more effective than others than in all prior centuries combined. I spent years studying effective churches that, compared to most other churches, reach a lot of people and influence the community around them. I discovered three practical questions that were especially useful in understanding some of the causes of church effectiveness: (1) What do the most effective churches *know* that other churches do not know, or at least do not take seriously? (2) What do the most effective churches *do* that most other churches do not do? (3) When effective churches do some of the same things that less effective churches do, *how* do they do them differently? I discovered that those issues—knowledge, actions, and style—matter more (in regard to outcomes) than most church leaders have ever imagined.

Twentieth-century scholars produced an impressive range of theories to account for organizational effectiveness. My field research confirmed that four of these theories substantially account for the effectiveness of churches, church organizations, denominations, and Christian movements. As one reflects upon them and works with them, one discovers that, as Kurt Lewin once assured us, "There is nothing more practical than a good theory."

1. The Mission Theory

Peter Drucker, the supreme guru of the twentieth-century management revolution, contended that the leaders of organizations need to be asking two questions frequently: (1) What is our main business? (2) How is business? Drucker believed that an organization's clarity regarding its purpose, mission, or main business is supremely important. If an organization's main business is clear, then it can define its several priority objectives, develop strategies for achieving those objectives, and devote human and physical resources to implementing the strategies. In Drucker's opus *Management: Tasks, Responsibilities, Practices* (Harper & Row, 1974), he demonstrated this theory's importance for businesses (like Sears), and also for the whole range of service institutions—such as governments, universities, hospitals, and churches.

Jim Collins, writing more recently in the Drucker tradition, recommended that organizations frame and articulate their mission in the form of a BHAG—a "Big Hairy Audacious Goal"![8] John Wesley's vision for eighteenth-century British Methodism, "To reform the nation and spread scriptural holiness across the land," qualifies as a BHAG. Likewise, Redeemer Presbyterian Church articulates its main business: "To spread the gospel, first through ourselves and then through the city, by word, deed, and community. To bring about personal changes, social healing, and cultural renewal through a movement of churches and ministries that change New York City and through it, the world."

2. The Culture Theory

Cultural anthropology—the study of the beliefs, values, symbols, and customs of human societies—was another field that blossomed in the twentieth century. Scholars studied cultures from specific microlevels, such as distinct tribes, to general macrolevels, such as Arabic or Nordic culture. The study of the culture concept had the effect of liberating the thinking of many people, for this reason: most human beings have been stuck in ethnocentrism for most of human history. In every society, we are so pervasively and unconsciously socialized into our society's ways and worldview, from such an early age, and our culture therefore seems so natural to us, that we observe another people's beliefs or customs as strange, if not bizarre or evil. But an understanding of Cultural Anthropology 101 helps us make new sense of another culture AND of our own. These studies have quietly educated an unprecedented number of informed world Christians.

By the early 1980s, students of organizations had discovered that *an organization* develops a distinctive culture (or subculture). So, for instance, people at IBM typically dress, act, talk, and work differently than people at Apple. Organizations as varied as Disney or Harvard or the New York Yankees can be understood in terms of certain distinctive symbols, values, traditions, and customs. Bringing new people into a culture-rich organization involves socializing them into the stories that embody the organization's core beliefs and values, and into an understanding of "how we do things around here."[9] In time, students of organizational culture emphasized two important keys to an organization's health and effectiveness: (1) The organization's core *values* must be clear, AND (2) its people must experience the leadership acting consistently with values they say they believe; perceived inconsistencies between the organization's values and practices breeds dysfunction and pathology, whereas *consistency* catalyzes health and effectiveness.

Some churches began using the culture concept to clarify and appraise their own characteristic beliefs, values, and practices. Before church leaders acquired the conceptual ability to distinguish between Christianity and culture, they usually assumed that whatever we believe, however we "do church," and however we live, is "Christianity." The folk logic was undeniable; we are Christians, so our beliefs, values, norms, and practices must be what Jesus and the apostles originally had in mind! We can now be clearer, however, that since people, organizations, societies, and denominational traditions are influenced by their surrounding culture, AND they construct their own organizational culture, AND they are infected with pride, selfishness, and other variants of humanity's sinful condition, our ways are not always God's ways. One day, this one insight could catalyze another Reformation.

3. The Involvement Theory

The human relations school of thought, led in the mid-twentieth century by Kurt Lewin, Douglas McGregor, and others, produced an indispensable perspective for leading people in organizations. You get people meaningfully involved, participating. When Lewin led race-relations training in Bethel, Maine, in the 1940s, he discovered that people learned and changed more through group participation than from passive learning. McGregor studied the assumptions about human nature that inhabited the minds of managers and supervisors. In *The Human Side of Enterprise* (McGraw-Hill, 1960), he challenged the prevailing "theory X" assumption about people—that most people in organizations are irresponsible and uncreative drones who need to be directed and even threatened to make them produce. He introduced an alternative "theory Y" paradigm about human nature: more people are capable, responsible, creative, and eager to contribute to the organization's success than most leaders assume, and the leaders who know this can lead the organization to achieve much more, especially in the long term.

The most important application of Lewin and McGregor's legacy emphasizes the power of participative leadership. When there are decisions to be made, problems to be solved, or a future to be planned, people often resist (or devote less than their full energy to) *imposed* decisions, solutions, and plans. If, however, leaders involve the people, the organization taps into a wider knowledge base and develops better decisions, solutions, and plans that are more likely to be "owned" by the people and are more likely to be implemented with full energy.

4. The Contextualization Theory

Scholars in the twentieth century also became clearer that organizations are not self-contained entities. They exist within a wider physical, historical, and cultural environment or context; they depend on that context in many ways; and, if the organization is achieving its mission, it is affecting that wider world. In other words, one reason an organization may be ineffective is that it functions as a "closed system"; an effective organization is an "open system."[10] At one level, the theory can be simply stated: the organization receives "inputs" from the environment, submits the inputs to "throughputs" (or "transformational activities"), and in time produces "outputs" into the wider community. A local church, for instance, receives new members, seekers, Bibles, music, staff, ideas, water, electricity, and many other "inputs" from the world around it. The church combines all of that into a range of intentional transformational activities like worship, Scripture study, small group experiences, counseling, and intercession. If the transformational activities are effective, the church is producing ideas, literature, ministries, causes, transformed people, and other outputs into the world, for the sake of the world.

One can see, from the open-system model, the importance of a church (or any organization) being relevant to the world around it—speaking its language, engaging its issues and struggles, and so on. In Christianity's world mission, we have long known to "indigenize" or "contextualize" the church's forms of ministry to fit the host population. We have heard, for a long time, that as the world around the church changes, the church must change too; but, in some quarters, this suggestion can quickly escalate into conflict.

The perennial issues center on what to change and what *not* to change. We have discovered in missiology four terms—message, mission, style, and strategy—that help us slice through this mountain of complexity. In broad terms, many of us commend the following two policies: (1) We are not called to change the *message*, because that is given in the gospel; we are often called to change the *style* in which we communicate the meaning of the message. (2) We are not called to change the *mission*, because that is mandated in Scripture; we are called to contextualize the *strategy* through which we pursue the mission's objectives in every mission field on earth.

I still meet church leaders who say that they do not believe in contextualization. I sometimes find myself replying, "Yes you do. If you preach or teach in a language other than Hebrew, Aramaic, or Greek, you believe in linguistic contextualization. And if you serve grape juice rather than fermented wine at the sacrament, you believe in contextualizing nonlinguistic symbols as well. You are continuing the contextualization decisions made by your predecessors in your tradition, but you are not yet making your own strategic decisions."

After suggesting that churches are organizations, we have rehearsed four theories—mission, culture, involvement, and contextualization—that substantially explain why some organizations (including churches) are more effective than other organizations. Many church leaders, however, are more interested in action than theory. They want to *do* something. So they want to know *what to do* to turn their church around. This "itch to act" is understandable; we want to make a difference.

Not All Interventions Are Created Equal

But organization theorists are not oblivious to this itch. They have studied the kinds of actions that are intended to make a difference, change organizations, and help organizations achieve their missions. They call such actions "interventions." They have studied interventions. They have identified an astonishing range of actions in which organization leaders have engaged to try to turn their organizations around. They have discovered that most interventions underachieve; not all interventions are created equal!

I was reminded of this one day when a friend sent me the following story by e-mail.

A county-seat town in Texas was subjected to a growing squirrel population, and hundreds of the squirrels decided to inhabit one or another of the town's five houses of worship. Leaders of each church—Presbyterian, Baptist, Methodist, Episcopal, and a Jewish synagogue—held meetings to deliberate their response to the squirrel invasion, and each church decided on a different intervention. The Presbyterians decided that the squirrel visitation might be the predestined will of God; so they did nothing. The Baptists gathered their squirrels and put them in the baptistery, expecting they would drown; but the squirrels multiplied. The Methodists transported a truckload of squirrels to a wilderness area and released them; but in several days they were back. The Episcopalians confirmed all of their 110 squirrels into membership (and thereby doubled their membership!); then they saw squirrels only on Christmas and Easter! The Jewish synagogue performed a ceremony in which they circumcised one squirrel; they never saw any squirrels after that!

In the face of *all* challenges, there are many things we *could* do, many interventions we *could* try. But our churches have already tried many things that did not deliver, haven't they? Over and over, we get people involved in doing something. Some people even get excited and, although the intervention gives the church a proverbial shot in the arm, there is little or no enduring change. From our experience it is reasonable to assume that in our quest to join our Lord in moving churches from tradition to mission, there are many possible actions that would promise more than they delivered. There are, however, two broad approaches to intervening in a church's history that, when well executed, have a strong and consistent track record.

Interventions in the Leadership of Change

We have said that because Jesus was both divine and human, his church is both a spiritual organism and a human organization. Like other organizations, churches are more effective when their mission is clear, when their culture is healthy, when they involve their people in decisions and planning, and when they strategically adapt to their changing context. When churches are declining and they face continued decline, there are many things they *could* do, but most interventions underperform. In addition to defining and remembering a clear mission, paying attention to clarity and consistency in the church's values, getting people involved, and frequently adapting to the changing context, I know of only two major types of interventions that are nearly adequate to the task in a wide range of churches.

Strategic Planning

A church's spiritual and organizational dynamics especially come together when leaders engage in strategic planning for their church's future. Strategic planning is the nearest thing to an "iron law" of Church Growth. I have studied churches for decades and, with some attempt at precision, I can state the following conclusion: I have never found a church that had an

- *informed* strategic plan
- that was *understood*
- AND *owned* by the people,
- AND was *being implemented,*

where the church was not growing.[11]

Strategic planning is not new. It has been widely available for a generation; but strategic thinking is a foreigner in at least 80 percent of our churches. Virtually all churches engage in *operational* planning; they decide *who* will do *what* by *when* for the worship service and other activities for next weekend, or for next Advent or Lent; they do the specific planning that the calendar mandates.

Most of our churches, however, have not planned their direction and destination for the next five or ten years. Why are most church leaders not developing and implementing a strategic plan? They have never learned the process, AND they have heard wrongly that the process is as complicated as brain surgery! It isn't. The essentials of the process can be unpacked in several pages, and if leaders rehearse it and work with it enough to internalize it, they will have acquired a skill for crafting a desirable future.

An understanding of strategic thinking and planning goes back many centuries. Some scholars suggest that such thinking originated in the lore of military leaders who had to deploy armies and navies, and physical resources like food and equipment, to advance their military objectives (*stratēgia* in classical Greek referred to "the art of the general"). Other scholars suggest that the mission orders of the Roman Catholic Church pioneered the leadership principles and strategic thinking that leaders in many fields now find indispensable. For example, more than 450 years ago, Ignatius of Loyola raised up the Jesuits who, in one generation, built schools and offered higher education on several continents. Today, the Jesuits's "twenty-one thousand professionals run two thousand institutions in more than a hundred countries."[12]

In the twentieth century, leaders in corporations, governments, and agriculture pioneered ways for more long-range comprehensive planning. In the early 1980s, George Keller's *Academic Strategy* initiated countless college and university executives in the mysteries of strategic thinking.[13] Keller's more recent case study of Elon College's move from decline and obscurity to growth and excellence, *Transforming a College*,[14] dramatizes what can presumably happen in *any* organization *if* the leaders take the strategic approach seriously enough for long enough. Most churches have not yet taken strategic planning as seriously as many colleges have, but there is no need to wait until our George Keller has stepped up.

◆　　◆　　◆　　◆

Many leaders have heard that strategic planning takes a very long time and involves an almost unmanageable number of steps, which have to be done in precise sequence. Actually, the process is neither that lengthy nor that tidy. For churches and other local voluntary organizations, a serious planning group can develop a very useful strategic plan in a season or so. There are only seven essential tasks; three are done early, and then the other four are done.

The process mandates that some things take place outside, and perhaps before, the planning meetings. For instance, (1) the selection of the members for a planning team should prioritize choosing people who affirm the church's tradition, AND who are open to innovation, AND who are already recognized and trusted as "influencers" in the church. (2) Membership should include at least one skilled individual who will need to gather the data that will inform the planning process. This task includes gathering statistics about, for example, the church's worship attendance, membership, and new Christians for each of the last ten years, AND the most important community demographic data and trends available from such sources as the most recent census, the superintendent of schools, the city manager, and the newspaper's city editor. This task also includes organizing the data into "intelligence"—an eight- to ten-page paper summarizing the most important facts and trends, in the church and in the community, which should inform the planning. (3) Members need to agree that the planning process is not the private concern of the planning group. The process is seriously collaborative and participatory at every stage. Planning group members fan out periodically and meet with every group in the church—sharing drafts of the group's thinking and welcoming perspectives and suggestions.

◆   ◆   ◆   ◆

Do These Three Things Early

1. *Identify the Key Result Areas.* Identify the key result areas (KRAs) in which the church wants better results than it is now experiencing, and in which the church believes that God wants better results. This step is more necessary psychologically than logically; it is not strictly necessary in strategic planning. But working at this level gets the committee reflecting together and, here, you are likely making explicit the areas of concern that prompted you to do strategic planning in the first place. You now identify four or five or six KRAs. (A church might decide, for instance, that it needs to increase worship attendance, reach more young families, reach people in the recovery community, get more members involved in ministries, and become less provincial and more involved in world mission.)

2. *Do a "SWOT Analysis."* After the planning group's members have read and reflected upon the "intelligence" paper that summarized the most relevant data about the church and the community (*and* have added their own informed perceptions), you then ask four questions. Regarding the church, (a) "What are our *strengths?*" (A group, for instance, might regard the church's music, facilities, and youth ministry as strengths.) Regarding the church, (b) "What are our *weaknesses?*" (A group might identify the church's available parking spaces, children's ministries, and outreach to pre-Christian people as weaknesses.) Regarding the community, (c) "What *opportunities* do we see?" (The group might identify new families moving into the community, available parking at the adjacent school, and a network of talented contemporary musicians.) Regarding the community, (d) "What *threats* do we see?" (The group might identify an unfriendly-to-religion city council, or the prospect of a factory closing, or some projected highway construction as plausible threats.) Many planning groups will perceive a "match" between a strength and an opportunity (like a match between strength in youth ministry and the opportunity of new families moving in) as an obvious opportunity for growth.

3. *Develop a Mission Statement.* We are not free, of course, to make a church's main business be whatever we would like. The mission of the people of God is revealed in Scripture, from God's promise (in Genesis 12) that Abraham's descendents would one

113

day bless the peoples of the earth, to the New Testament's mandate for Christ's "ambassadors" (2 Corinthians 5) to communicate the gospel to—and make disciples among—the earth's peoples (Matthew 28:19-20). This mission is dramatized throughout the book of the Acts of the Apostles, and Jesus promised that the Holy Spirit would empower us for this mission. Our mission is revealed. It is not up to us. It is not even negotiable.

Nevertheless, a church's people need the experience of expressing that mission in their own words, adapted perhaps to the strengths of the church or the opportunities in the wider community, and to the indigenous language of the community. In cooperation with the involvement theory, leaders should involve everyone in this exercise, and should write and refine many drafts until the statement shines like a gem. The most effective mission statements are:

Simple
General
Imaginative
Energizing
Brief

(If the mission statement stretches much more than thirty words, it becomes less of a statement and more of an essay!) The ultimate test of the final draft is that it be *memorable*. Everyone needs to have it rehearsed and available in consciousness; otherwise, it is unlikely to serve as the church's compass pointing toward a destination that the church is likely to reach. Even with all of that, the people will need to be reminded at least monthly of "our main business"; without communication redundancy, people tend to forget, and the church slides toward maintaining the past rather than seeking the future that God wants for the church and the community.

The target audience for a mission statement is the church's leaders and people, but it is useful to have a statement that communicates with outsiders AND that models for church people the language that may communicate in the world. In some churches, this may not be politically possible; the supporters who haven't sorted out the relationship between symbols and meanings still need to hear the language of Zion or they fear that their church has "lost the faith." The mission statement of Southeast Christian Church in Louisville, Kentucky, while internally useful, may reflect such pressures: "Southeast Christian Church exists to

evangelize the lost,
edify the saved,
minister to those in need, and
be a conscience in the community."

The mission statement that drove Shepherd of the Valley Lutheran Church in Phoenix, Arizona, in the 1970s and 1980s, was more broadly and powerfully suggestive: "To know Him and to make Him known." In that same period, Willow Creek Community Church, in the northwest sector of metropolitan Chicago, crystallized a purpose that has served them ever since: "To help irreligious people become fully devoted followers of Jesus Christ."

In *Leading and Managing a Growing Church*, I suggested:

> The purpose for developing a mission statement is, quite simply, to determine the organization's identity, supreme purpose, major direction, and essential mission for, say, the next five years. A strong mission statement will become the "driving force" of the organization, shaping decisions, impacting budget priorities, and keeping the church on course over time.... Its function is to shape and drive the priorities, decisions, and activities of the organization's people.[15]

Then Do Three More Things

4. From your mission statement, *identify the more specific objectives (and goals) that you intend to achieve*. Your objectives *may* be implied in the mission statement. Shepherd of the Valley Church's mission statement ("To know Him and to make Him known"), for instance, suggests two objectives: (1) to know Him, and (2) to make Him known. The church, however, developed four objectives. They wanted to help people:

1. Get right (to know and experience their justification)

2. Grow right (to root people in Scripture, theology, and Christianity's ethic)

3. Go right (to involve people in ministry, evangelism, and mission)

4. Glow right (to involve people in ongoing spiritual formation)

Planners should work to clarify a manageable range of objectives (four, five, or six) for the church's future. The group may revisit the key result areas, identified in the first step, to move toward stating some of the objectives.

Once the church's objectives are reasonably clear, the planners will need to *attach* at least one *goal* to each objective. Many writers suggest that effective goals tend to be *specific, attainable,*[16] and *measurable*. Some writers add the criterion of *ownership*; goals are enormously more likely to be achieved if the people own them; their ownership comes through (and not without) involving people in the goal setting. Occasionally, writers add that effective goals are *scheduled*; the milestones toward their planned achievement are written on the calendar. The goals, of course, are not as important as the objectives to which they are attached; but the goals are specific indicators of whether you are achieving your objectives.

5. The next step is to identify the broad *strategies* that will move the church toward the attainment of its objectives. Within a church or mission's evangelization objectives, the Church Growth field has identified certain broad strategic directions we observe in Christian movements, such as: (a) Identify and reach receptive people and groups while they are receptive. (b) Reach out and invite across the social networks of your committed people, and especially to the friends and relatives of your new converts. (c) Reach some of the "impossible" or "hopeless" groups of people in the community; when some of them are reached, those apparent miracles will catalyze receptivity in many other people.[17] (d) Do not count on your current established

groups, congregations, and ministries to reach all or even most of the people your church could reach. *New* units and expressions are disproportionately reproductive; much growth takes place through, and not without, the proliferation of groups, congregations, and ministries.

6. The final step is to identify the specific *programs*, *ministries*, and *activities* through which the church will express the strategies that will help achieve the objectives of their mission. If, for example, the church wants to reach a new generation of young couples with children, new Sunday school classes might help reach and involve many of them. If a church wants to reach a range of people with addictions, then a range of twelve-step ministries are a proven programmatic expression.[18]

With this step, the strategic planning process is essentially completed—although the leaders should revisit, revise, and improve the strategic plan at least annually. Each time that an updated strategic plan is in place, "operational planning" then takes over. Most churches are already experienced in asking, "Who needs to do what by when?"

"What If Our Church Isn't Ready for Strategic Planning?"

At any given time, some churches are not ready to engage in strategic thinking about their future. They may have just welcomed a new pastor; they may be in between pastors. They may be managing a crisis that now consumes priority attention and energy. They may be consumed with activities that they enjoy (although they have likely forgotten what those activities were supposed to achieve in the lives of people). It may be all they can do to keep an inherited liturgy half-alive, or to get through Lent, or even to get through next weekend. Or they may not now face the future with much hope, so the intervention they need right now is more spiritual than organizational. Or they may resist the self-examination that would reveal the church's strengths and (especially) weaknesses. Or they may have heard, from someone in their grapevine, that strategic planning is "no longer trendy."[19]

Some churches say they are ready for change, but they say they would rather do "something else" than plan for their long-range future. For such churches, I am the reporter of bad news. Most of the interventions that churches like to engage in do not, and cannot, make much difference. A problem, after all, has a cause. (Actually, most problems have multiple causes!) An intervention needs to address a problem's main cause in order to substantially solve the problem. For that reason, at least, not all of the possible interventions are created equal.

In the face of continued membership decline, a church has many choices—but few would make much difference. As I have already suggested, the range of interventions in churches that could substantially help move a church from tradition to mission is astonishingly limited. The statement etched in granite across the front of Boston's Prudential building is probably true: "The future belongs to those who prepare for it." Robert Schuller's slogan has proven truer than anyone wishes were the case: "If you fail to plan, you plan to fail." Leaders with an informed plan in place—a plan owned by the people—and implementing the plan, are in time light-years ahead of where they would have been without planning their future. There is no more proven approach to the future than to plan your work and then work your plan.

There is, however, a promising option for a church with an inferiority complex (or a church that has, for any reason, an allergy to planning). Many churches, from whatever history of experiences, have such low group self-esteem that they are not secure enough to engage in the "diagnosis" phase of the strategic planning process—that phase in which they would identify, face, and deal with the church's weaknesses; and such churches also assume (falsely) that their church has no strengths upon which they could build a desirable future. For such churches, I am confident of one alternative to strategic planning.

"Breakthrough Projects" for Turning It Around

Robert Schaffer, a psychologist and organization consultant, pioneered an alternative way to help insecure, unhealthy, low self-esteem, even depressed organizations experience a turnaround. He called it the "breakthrough project."[20] Until I read Schaffer, I had noticed that many effective churches could report a history of important projects that stimulated growth, but I had not yet made the causal connection that the project approach could catalyze turnarounds in declining churches. Once I put on Schaffer's eyeglasses, I could perceive the pattern in the histories of many churches that were once declining and were now growing.

The breakthrough project approach to an organization begins with discovering *something* (almost anything) that the organization's people are already itching to see done. In churches, the most obvious incipient project may relate to their physical facility—such as the need to fix the steps or to put a new roof on the outhouse! Fixing the steps will not, as an isolated project, make much enduring difference. Schaffer's key to change is to *begin* with a project the people are ready for, and then make that project the first in a *series of projects* that, incrementally, moves the church toward a more desirable future while consciously learning together, from the project experiences, to become a more achieving organization. A series of projects focuses the people's energy, harnesses their skills and abilities, and gets them pulling together to achieve something important and visible in measurable time. The following "Top Ten Guidelines" are probably indispensable:

1. For the first project (and each project), choose a project many of the people are ready, willing, and able to do; that requires no funds or skills or authority beyond those already available; and that would require no more than a season to achieve. Choose a project that, when achieved, would be a visible success.

2. Put a capable person (or team) in charge who "owns" the project, who can lead and manage the project.

3. Define the project's *objectives*, the periodic *milestones* toward achieving the objectives, and the *scheduling* of each milestone's achievement.

4. Divide the project into *tasks* and define who will need to achieve each task by when.

5. Determine and allocate the *resources*—the personnel, time, funds, equipment, and facilities that will be needed for each task.

6. Throughout the project, remind people of the purpose the project is serving and keep communicating its progress to each work unit and to the church.

7. When the project is finished, have a public celebration and rehearse what you did. One of your purposes is to change the organization's culture—the shared understanding of "the way we do things around here."

8. With the momentum of several successes, and the people's increasing confidence, competence, and new shared way of working together, take on larger projects.

9. Choose projects that would advance the long-range objectives of the organization, as those become defined.

10. In time, when the congregation has regained some momentum and self-esteem, put the project orientation more clearly within the service of a strategic plan.

Robert Schaffer believed that the organization that follows and learns from the project-breakthrough approach can "make miracles routine."[21]

Six More Principles for Leading Change in Churches

In addition to spiritual and organizational perspectives for understanding effective churches, and strategic planning and breakthrough projects for moving churches from business as usual to their main business, experiences in many churches have revealed several rather specific "laws" for leading and managing change.

1. Dissatisfaction

Early in a change effort, leaders will probably need to uncork or produce some conscious and shared *dissatisfaction* with the status quo. Since satisfied members are not motivated to change anything, it may be necessary to catalyze some dissatisfaction. (While many church leaders spend their careers trying to minimize dissatisfaction, strategic planning is not the time for risk aversion or smoothing over people's feelings.) This is often done in two ways:

A. Give the leadership group the membership data (such as worship attendance, number of converts, and year-end membership) for each of the last ten years. Get them involved with the data by graphing the data, and then have them project (on the same graph) where the trends will be ten years from now—if the church does not change. Then ask them if that is where they want the church to be ten years from now. *If* they say no, have them indicate on the graph where they want the church to be. The difference between where the church is going and where they want the church to go is the "planning gap." Identifying and experiencing that gap will often induce a season of dissatisfaction.

B. Take a vanload of people on a "pilgrimage" to another church, in a similar context and opportunity, that is achieving and growing much more than your church. As your people experience a more apostolic congregation, learn what they did strategically, meet and hear some of their converts, and visualize what is possible, they will want to replicate something like this "back home."

2. Affirmation

It is always faithful, usually useful, and often necessary to *affirm* the church's past and what God has done in the church's past, and to show how the proposed changes represent *continuity* with the past.

118

Many people initially interpret a change proposal as a possible belittling of the church's past and all that God was once doing when the church was planted, or when the sanctuary was built, or "when Pastor Jones was here." So historical reality and current strategy converge when leaders *emphasize* that we stand, gratefully, and build on the foundations of the past; and *if* we can now see farther than our predecessors did, it is because we stand on the shoulders of those who have gone before us. Since the world has changed, we honor our forebears by bringing the same devout entrepreneurial imagination to our challenge that they brought to theirs.

We are in continuity with the past because our mission is the same as theirs, though our strategy in service of that mission needs to change so we can engage the changed community. Furthermore, our message has not changed, but the style in which we express it *does* need to change to engage the unchurched people who do not understand the old religious language.

Consider a case. A church's leaders decided that, in addition to the church's traditional service, they needed to add a more contemporary "seeker service" to reach pre-Christian people. The new service would be informal, and would introduce "Christianity 101" in the language and style of the target audience, and would feature culturally current Christian music. To "sell" the members on the faithfulness and wisdom of this proposal, the leaders "positioned" the new service in the lineage of the old Sunday evening service, which had served their denominational tradition and had reached many people for more than a century, before it wound down. The Sunday evening service, for its time, introduced Christianity in a more casual context, in language and music that was then current. "The seeker service has the same DNA," they explained. "We are proposing an updated version of the old Sunday evening service—for Sunday mornings!"

3. Reminding the People

Periodically, *remind people* of three facts:

A. Remind the people that there are no unchanging churches. When members die or move away or when new members join, when a pastor leaves and a new pastor arrives, or when the economy changes or the community changes, the church experiences change—whether anticipated or not, desired or not.

B. Lest the congregation's "Chicken Littles" panic and fear that the sky is falling, "anchor" the people by reminding them of all the things that will *not* change. They will have the same property, the same sanctuary, the same staff, the same traditional service, and especially the same mission and message.

C. Remind the people that during the innovation's implementation period they will likely experience *discomfort*. If the leaders do not warn them, when the people experience discomfort they may blame the leaders! If the leaders do inoculate them against the discomfort to come, the people will experience less discomfort than they expected, and they may even have some fun at the leaders' expense!

4. Critiquing "What We Have Always Done"

A change effort will likely have to consider abandoning long-standing programs and activities that are no longer effective in reaching people or discipling people, or are no longer achieving any other worthy objective. George Odiorne once observed that, sooner or later, most organizations become stuck in "the activity trap."[22] He explained that organizations typically begin with a clear vision of what they intend to achieve, and they organize people into a range of activities in which they pull together to achieve the organization's mission; the activities are the organization's means for achieving the mission's goals.

Over time (years or decades), however, the people's understanding of the mission becomes hazy, and the activities become ritualized and misunderstood as ends in themselves. So, for instance, a declining church may report that they have "always been organized like this"; worship has "always" been scheduled at 10:45; the church has "always" scheduled the spring rummage sale, the summer Vacation Bible School, and the fall revival; the published devotional guide has "always" been distributed to each member on the first Sunday of each quarter; the youth have always scheduled a winter ski retreat; and the Ladies Mission Guild still meets monthly—but no one can remember when it last supported much mission! At this point, Odiorne contended, the organization is in serious need of renewal.

One problem with many inherited programs and activities (in addition to their lost productivity) is that they take up space and time, and they usually require financial support and staff time. It may cost more time, energy, and money to perpetuate something "after its time" than what it cost when it had momentum. Peter Drucker emphasized that organizations that need renewal and recovery of their main business often need to appraise everything they have been doing for a long time. Leaders, he said, need to ask of every traditional program and activity, "If we were not already doing this, would we choose to start doing it now?" By jettisoning programs that once worked but no longer do we liberate time, space, staff, and energy for new programs, activities, and ministries than can gather harvests.

5. Pilot Programs

Present almost every change proposal as a *pilot program*. Many people dread supporting an innovation that they will be "stuck with forever" if it doesn't work. There are, of course, some proposals—like relocation or a new facility—that will be in place for as long as anyone can anticipate. But most new program and activity proposals, such as a 9:00 a.m. seeker service, a recovery ministry, helping a new church get planted, involvement in Habitat for Humanity, or buying textbooks for a mission school, *can* and should be ended when the objectives are achieved *or* if God does not bless the program and it cannot achieve its objectives. If we present our great new idea as a pilot project, and if we schedule the date on which it will be evaluated, and if on that date we do honestly evaluate it, the people will become *much* more open to change and innovation in the future.

6. Change More by Addition than Subtraction

When most church leaders hear someone proposing mission achievement through change, they usually *hear* the advocate advising them to change the traditional 11:00 worship service AND to change the traditional people who attend it. That would be, in Machiavelli's memorable words, a leadership challenge that is "difficult to take in hand," AND "perilous to conduct," AND "uncertain in its success"! No wonder pastors are often reluctant to consider a change effort!

A careful rereading of this material, however, will turn up no instance in which I recommend changing a traditional congregation and its people, as Plan A, or B, or even C or D. Dale Galloway has often counseled pastors, in situations where the church could reach more people, to develop a "two-track church." Do *not* try to change the satisfied traditional congregation that you have inherited. Serve them faithfully while building, "at the edge," an alternative congregation based on cultural relevance, emotional relevance, small groups, lay ministries, outreach ministries, and world mission. (Then, in time, you may proliferate a third alternative congregation, and a fourth, and so on.) "You serve the traditional congregation," Galloway suggests, "to fund the future." You start the alternative congregation "to *have* a future."

Postscript

Sometimes, when a church's people have seen a more apostolic way forward, they *still* do not take that way. They have rediscovered what their forebears once knew: that we are entrusted with the gospel for the sake of people who are not reconciled, restored, redeemed, and redeployed followers of Jesus Christ. They comprehend, much more clearly than before, how to "do church" in a missionary context and how to expand their church's reach locally and globally. They now know how to discover *who* to reach and *how* to reach them. They even know what is involved in moving a church from tradition to mission. The leaders and people are more convinced than ever that it should be done, and they understand how it could be done, but they do not get around to doing it. (They are analogous to people who learn the role of aerobic and anaerobic exercise in achieving health and fitness, and they even pick up some of the jargon—such as "intervals" and "intensity"—but the health club considers them AWOL, and they are as sedentary and out of shape as before.)

For years, I wondered *why*? Once the people have rediscovered the gospel that can change the world and they have glimpsed the apostolic adventure that is enormously more fulfilling than merely attending church and serving on committees, they are still stuck. One reason is widely known. Most organizations, following *any* intervention in the organization's life, will probably revert back to the old ways unless the new ways are institutionalized. "The way we have always done it" affects most church people like gravity pulling them back into the patterns of the past.

I think I have discovered two more reasons, and I discovered them, from churches that *did* move from tradition to mission, when I asked them, "What almost kept you from doing it?"

(1) Often, church leaders said that they were reluctant to take the risks. They liked the feeling of being in control, and they knew that we control what happens much more in our facility than if we engage the community's people on their turf. Furthermore, these church leaders were reluctant to put their members "at risk." They had negative fantasies about losing some of their members to "the world."

Regarding those two anxieties around the risk factor, we have gained some wisdom. First, we are less in control when we are in ministry beyond the church facility, but churches that defy their anxiety, and do it anyway, discover that ministry in the world is more interesting and energizing, and they find themselves depending more on the Holy Spirit! They now experience the reality of being the salt and the light that penetrates the world; of being like the sower who "goes forth" to scatter the seed, and later entering the harvest to gather it; and they experience the meaning of being "ambassadors for Christ."

Second, a church's life in the world *does* involve some risk of losing their people to the world. Jesus dramatized this risk in the parable of the lost sheep, in which the shepherd leaves the gathered flock "in the wilderness" (*not* safely "in the fold" as the old hymn misremembers) while he searches for the lost sheep. Churches *do* experience the risk of losing people; with some regularity, church members "revert to the world" and, in time, their names are removed from the membership roll. We have learned, however, that tamed-down traditional churches put their members at *much* greater risk than the churches that deploy their people in ministry and witness in the world. (The members of very traditional churches often never experience the adventure of actually following Jesus in the world; in such churches, many members have one eye on the exit.) Furthermore, we vastly exaggerate the power of the world's temptations for drawing people out of the church's life, compared to the quiet expelling power of the routine in low-expectation traditional churches. Actually, *if* the church does outreach ministry from the life of Christian community, and *if* they penetrate the world in teams, and *if* they intercede for one another, and *if* they process each experience together, their people typically discover that the world's alleged allures are idols that offer nothing compared to life in the kingdom of God.

(2) Again, when I have asked church leaders, "What almost kept you from becoming missional?" I heard a second reason that surely stops many other churches from proceeding. They had resisted because they thought that the life of outreach would move them beyond their comfort zone, but they convinced themselves that they could "feel comfortable" doing outreach ministry and witness after all.

That conclusion is a delusion! The truth of the matter is that in crucial conversations and other ministries, as "friends of sinners" in the world, the stakes are so high for the other person that we never become fully adequate for this ministry; so that we often function out of our comfort zones. While the discomfort diminishes enough with experience that it loses its threat to immobilize us, we never really "graduate." Indeed, if Christians *ever* get to the point where they can evangelize as casually as asking directions, that is a sign that they should no longer do it. People, after all, are more likely to sense the revelation being mediated through us *when* they perceive our discomfort; and when they sense that we care about them enough to experience discomfort while helping them, they are more likely to respond.

The issue is *not* whether we will always feel comfortable in outreach. (Where did the idea ever come from, that we are only supposed to do what we feel comfortable doing?) The issue *is* whether we will depend on the Spirit and the community of faith enough to defy any feelings of discomfort, and whether we care enough and dare enough to experience discomfort for their sakes. Being an ambassador for Christ may even involve tasting some of the agony of Gethsemane.

Not long ago, in the city where we live, the local newspaper reported an event that can serve all Christians as a parable.[23] Following a heavy rain, a truck deliveryman and associate pastor named Wayne Stevenson noticed a frantic mother duck near a storm sewer and he sensed that her babies had been swept into the underground sewer. That night, he said, "I couldn't get it out of my mind or out of my heart. They are God's creatures." He returned to the sewer opening the next day. The mother Mallard was no longer there, but he heard a "peep" from one opening. He lifted a manhole cover and managed to rescue one exhausted duckling; he lifted another cover and reached two more.

He was unable to reach two others, so his wife Karen telephoned the Lexington Animal Care and Control office for help, and the office sent Elizabeth Gehlbach. She captured a fourth duckling, but to reach the fifth she had to crawl on her stomach through a narrow sewer pipe. Gehlbach knew the babies would need an adoptive mother, so she drove them to the lake at Lexington Cemetery, where many candidates for the job would be present. When she turned the ducklings loose, they followed a flock of adult ducks into the lake.

The next day, Elizabeth Gehlbach commented to a reporter, "I feel pretty confident that they got adopted out there." Then she reflected on her experience in rescuing the fifth duckling. "I was inching my way along the drain. It wasn't very fun because I'm claustrophobic, and there were a lot of spiders and I'm also arachnophobic."

If *we* ever decide that *our* fears or discomfort will no longer restrain us from reaching lost people who need to be found, Christianity will become a contagious movement across the land.

NOTES

Preface
1. C. S. Lewis, *Mere Christianity* (San Francisco: HarperCollins, 2001), 199.

1. (Re)Introducing Church Growth to a New Generation
1. For a recent and magisterial interpretation of this complex history, see Charles Taylor, *A Secular Age* (Cambridge, Mass.: Belknap Press, 2007).

2. Donald A. McGavran and Win Arn, *How To Grow a Church* (Glendale, Calif.: Regal Books, 1973).

3. See Arthur G. McPhee, *The Road to Delhi: Bishop Pickett Remembered, 1890–1981* (Bangalore: SAIACS Press, 2005). McPhee's reflection on Pickett's life and contribution is comprehensive and perceptive, an excellent mission biography.

4. Donald A. McGavran, *The Bridges of God: A Study in the Strategy of Missions* (New York: Friendship Press, 1955).

5. Some readers will notice that Christian Schwarz's name is not in that list. His *Natural Church Development* is not a Church Growth book (though it claims to be). He focuses almost exclusively upon increasing the "health" of the existing church, which, as I explain later in this chapter, is only one of the six ways that churches grow. *Natural Church Development* represents a fairly traditional European state-church orientation much more than a missional or apostolic agenda.

6. Their referent for "theology" usually includes knowledge of Scripture as well as theology. Sometimes "theology" is meant to include theological ethics; sometimes it is meant to include only Bible. I once heard the C.E.O. of a mission agency say, "All missionaries need to know is the Bible."

7. One day McGavran mused that the World Council of Churches member churches had "hijacked" the mission that was bound for Jerusalem, to redirect it toward Philadelphia—the City of Brotherly Love. He mused, "The plane called 'mission' was actually bound for Philadelphia—with Jerusalem as the first stop!" He believed that "the *Christian* plane can only get to Philadelphia via Jerusalem." He pointed out that since the World Council of Churches' perspective took over the mission boards of many denominations, "they are no nearer to Philadelphia today than when they first took over."

8. Donald A. McGavran, *The Eye of the Storm* (Waco, Tex.: Word Press, 1972). The controversy continued on a global scale, so McGavran updated his advocacy in *The Conciliar-Evangelical Debate: The Crucial Documents, 1964–1976: Expanded Edition of The Eye of the Storm: The Great Debate in Mission, Including Documents on Bangkok and Nairobi* (South Pasadena, Calif.: William Carey Library, 1977). The Church Growth Movement, of course, was not the sole source of the period's controversies. McGavran and others were often engaging the many issues that swirled around mission. Mission's conciliar challengers often adopted the entire range of possible positions—from the position that mission should no longer be done at all to the position that "everything we do is mission!"

9. Donald A. McGavran, *Understanding Church Growth*, rev. ed. (Grand Rapids: Eerdmans, 1980), 100.

10. C. Peter Wagner, ed., *Church Growth: State of the Art* (Wheaton, Ill.: Tyndale House Publishers, 1986), 292, 298.

11. George G. Hunter III, *To Spread the Power: Church Growth in the Wesleyan Spirit* (Nashville: Abingdon Press, 1987), 32.

12. Christian A. Schwarz, *Natural Church Development: A Guide to Eight Essential Qualities of Healthy Churches* (Carol Stream, Ill.: ChurchSmart Resources, 1996). Schwarz and his team of German church leaders surveyed one thousand churches in thirty countries. They crunched the numbers and claimed "scientific" warrants for NCD's conclusions. Church Growth people and sociologists of religion view his project with dubiety, however. Schwarz and his team surveyed thirty *core members* of each of the one thousand churches. The problem is that core member perceptions may be subjective and atypical; for example, they may experience their church as more "loving" than would a first-time visitor who is a single mother with an addiction and a reputation. Furthermore, Schwarz's eight conclusions largely ratify what church leaders already knew. Who did not already know that "inspiring worship" would contribute to a church's health?

Again, some of us are embarrassed by NCD's omissions. In missiology, we have learned that churches need to contextualize everywhere to be effective in their mission; Schwarz dismisses missiology's most consensual and enduring strategic insight. Again, several decades after the Third Reich, we are astonished that some German church leaders *still* assume that a church can ignore justice and still be "healthy"! Some churches that slept through the rise of Nazism were, undoubtedly, healthy by Schwarz's criteria. How healthy can that be? Finally, Schwarz's advocates are confident that "natural church development has taken the place of church growth." Since, however, NCD *only* addresses internal growth, the claim is fatuous.

13. Schwarz, for some reason, contends that his adjectives are more important than his nouns—an assertion that merits two comments. (1) Does anyone really believe that "inspiring" is more important than "worship," or that "need-oriented" is more important than "evangelism"? Actually, most, if not all, of the nouns are far more important than the adjectives. (2) NCD's attachment of one, and only one, adjective to each noun is an oversimplification. Truth is seldom that simple, and what is going on is seldom that singular. For instance, leadership studies are clear that it is as important for leaders to be "visionary" as it is to be "empowering," and surely being "obedient" is as important in spirituality as being "passionate." It is more strategic to emphasize the nouns and to nuance each noun with one or several adjectives that will do fuller justice to the characteristic than one adjective alone can do.

14. George G. Hunter III, *The Celtic Way of Evangelism: How Christianity Can Reach the West . . . Again* (Nashville: Abingdon Press, 2000), 49-51.

15. See Reginald Johnson, *Your Personality and the Spiritual Life* (Gainesville, Fla.: Center for Applications of Psychological Type, 1999).

16. Church leaders may adapt the following guidelines to their context—to be set lower for a resistant context, higher for a receptive context.

17. Rodney Stark, "Efforts to Christianize Europe, 400–2000," *Journal of Contemporary Religion* 16, no. 1 (January 2001): 118.

18. See Timothy J. Keller and J. Allen Thompson, *Church Planter Manual* (New York: Redeemer Presbyterian Church, 2002), 12.

19. The Center's excellent 250-page *Church Planter Manual* is available from the church's online store (www.redeemer2.com/rstore/). The Center's motto is "Renewing Cities around the World through Church Planting."

20. Timothy Keller, *The Reason for God: Belief in an Age of Skepticism* (New York: Dutton, 2008). The book was published in February 2008. By late November, Amazon.com's readers had posted 130 customer reviews.

21. Timothy Keller, *The Prodigal God: Recovering the Heart of the Christian Faith* (New York: Dutton, 2008).

22. Redeemer's curriculum for developing fellowship group leaders is also available from the

church's online store (www.redeemer2.com/rstore/). It can be purchased and downloaded at a modest cost.

23. Michael Luo, "Preaching the Word and Quoting the Voice: An Evangelist Thrives in Manhattan by Embracing the City and Identifying with Its Culture," *New York Times*, 26 February 2006, New York Report sec., p. 28.

2. What Kind of Church Reaches Pre-Christian People?

1. C. S. Lewis, *Mere Christianity* (San Francisco: HarperCollins, 2001), 199.

2. Martha Grace Reese, *Unbinding the Gospel: Real Life Evangelism* (St. Louis: Chalice Press, 2006).

3. See my three books, *How to Reach Secular People* (Nashville: Abingdon Press, 1992), chapter 6; *Church for the Unchurched* (Nashville: Abingdon Press, 1996); and *Radical Outreach: The Rediscovery of Apostolic Ministry and Evangelism* (Nashville: Abingdon Press, 2003).

4. I first heard Bruce Larson announce these correlations in the early 1980s and subsequent field research has validated them.

5. I have developed these themes more thoroughly in *The Celtic Way of Evangelism* (Nashville: Abingdon Press, 2000), and in *Radical Outreach*.

6. One book has, for many Christian leaders, delineated the almost manageable range of interventions that help impoverished peoples get to the first step. See Jeffrey D. Sachs, *The End of Poverty: Economic Possibilities for Our Time* (New York: Penguin Books, 2005).

7. See Donald E. Miller and Tetsunao Yamamori, *Global Pentecostalism: The New Face of Christian Social Engagement* (Berkeley: University of California Press, 2007).

8. I have expanded on the recovery of evangelical Christianity's social mandate in *Christian, Evangelical, & . . . Democrat?* (Nashville: Abingdon Press, 2006).

9. Miller and Yamamori, *Global Pentecostalism*, 60.

10. Art Beals was University Presbyterian Church's Minister of Missions throughout most of Larson's tenure. Beals shared what they learned in *When the Saints Go Marching Out: Mobilizing the Church for Mission* (Louisville, Ky.: Geneva Press, 2001).

11. Dean M. Kelley, *Why Conservative Churches Are Growing: A Study in the Sociology of Religion* (New York: HarperCollins, 1972).

3. Perspectives on Relevant Christianity

1. In the decades that I have worked with this issue, my assumptions have been challenged hundreds of times.

2. This exposé should reveal why it really is difficult for church leaders to please everyone! My discussion to follow will begin by siding with the last group or two but will eventually affirm the other points of view by showing that relevance *only* to the young or to the unchurched will prevent them, once we reach them, from ever experiencing the range, depth, roots, and expanding appreciation that characterizes *all* maturing Christian disciples. One other type of church should be mentioned. Some traditions intend to reconnect with *one feature* that they believe characterized early Christianity, such as worshiping in homes or on Saturday or without music instruments; but, in most other ways, they share the agenda of one of the other traditions, such as keeping nineteenth-century music and language alive. They may experience, then, some of the same issues, such as whether to change anything to keep younger people or engage unchurched people.

3. The most influential text is Dan Sperber and Deirdre Wilson, *Relevance: Communication and Cognition*, 2nd ed. (Oxford: Blackwell, 1995). This field of study is one of an astonishing range of specific fields within the broad communication umbrella. The field is positioned

somewhere in the region of semiotics and pragmatics. By the way, Christians are not the only people who sometimes fail to practice what they preach. You would reasonably expect a text in communication to communicate, but *Relevance* is a laboriously difficult read.

4. I believe that Sperber and Wilson make a convincing case for the existence of an inferential principle within human beings; and demonstrated relevance does, indeed, seem to have the power to engage this capacity. I observe this capacity possibly surfacing every semester when, as I am teaching something, a student asks, "Professor Hunter, will this be on the final exam?" I have mentioned that most of the relevance theory literature that I have tackled is written at a high level of abstraction that makes for difficult reading; this is my attempt at a *Reader's Digest* version. My summary in these paragraphs, especially the four key words—*adapting, connecting, engaging,* and *interesting*—is entirely my own construction, for which Sperber and Wilson should not be blamed!

5. Occasionally, this may involve siding with them more than with the church. One man recently declared, "Whatever else Jesus was, he was the Prince of Peace, so churches should not be so gung ho for war." Fidelity to the Christian revelation required me to agree. I said, "We need more people like you, who know this and take it seriously, in our churches."

6. Within the rhetorical communication field, the most influential theme of the twentieth century was Kenneth Burke's case that identification may play a more prominent role in public influence than Aristotle's long-reigning emphasis upon persuasion. Burke observed the alienation that afflicts human relations and human affairs, and he taught that the influential advocate will identify and empathize with the background, worldview, experiences, and interests of the target population. See Kenneth Burke, *A Rhetoric of Motives* (Berkeley: University of California Press, 1969).

7. Yes, in a weak moment I trolled the Internet for relevance quotations. I found this one at www.brainyquote.com.

8. See Donald A. McGavran, *Understanding Church Growth*, 3rd ed. (Grand Rapids: Eerdmans, 1990), 289-93, for his most recent delineation of these stages; but my discussion draws from other sources, especially from his *Ethnic Realities and the Church: Lessons from India* (Pasadena, Calif.: William Carey Library, 1979), and from the way he used to discuss the stages.

9. McGavran, *Understanding Church Growth*, 290.

10. Indeed, the younger church's leaders may even divide into factions and fight over the inheritance.

11. The sending nation, for instance, may experience financial recession. Or a rising generation of denominational leaders may change the denomination's priorities. Much mission support is catalyzed by identification with missionaries known and loved by people in the pew. With fewer missionaries serving that field and fewer missionaries interpreting that field to donors, and with the sending church now identifying with fewer missionaries in that field, in time the sending church invests less in that field. Furthermore, the national leaders of the young church may change some policies or do some things differently than the missionaries did. The national leaders may even make some mistakes. Earlier, the missionaries made mistakes, but the mission's promotional reports and literature engaged in less than full disclosure!

12. McGavran, *Understanding Church Growth*, 291.

13. Ibid., 292. In this paragraph, McGavran was explicit about the first and third tracks. He featured the second track elsewhere.

14. Drawing from and adapting categories from cultural anthropology, Ralph Winter influenced the Church Growth Movement to think in terms of "modality" and "sodality." The modality refers to regular parish or diocesan Christianity—communities of Christians and seekers gathered for worship in any of the first three types of community discussed in this section. The sodality refers to the fourth type—movements and organizations of Christians who have a

focused passion, who share an advanced commitment, and who gain advanced specialized knowledge that informs their cause. See Ralph Winter's influential essay "The Two Structures of God's Redemptive Mission" in *Perspectives on the World Christian Movement: A Reader*, ed. Ralph D. Winter and Steven C. Hawthorne (Pasadena, Calif.: William Carey Library, 1999).

15. This reflection is *not* an implied argument that a younger church has nothing to learn anymore from Western theology. Indeed, the experience of learning from one another's experience and insight is one of the enormous privileges of being a world Christian. Such learning is multidirectional, however, and we are clearly past the time that Western theologians can even pretend to do *all* of the theological reflection for the church in all of the earth's cultural regions.

16. On this supremely important topic, Paul Hiebert's *Transforming Worldviews: An Anthropological Understanding of How People Change* (Grand Rapids: Baker Academic, 2008) takes the place of the book we never had before.

17. See George G. Hunter III, *To Spread the Power: Church Growth in the Wesleyan Spirit* (Nashville: Abingdon Press, 1987), chapter 7; *Church for the Unchurched* (Nashville: Abingdon Press, 1996), chapter 3; and *Radical Outreach: The Recovery of Apostolic Ministry and Evangelism* (Nashville: Abingdon Press, 2003), chapter 3. My *Celtic Way of Evangelism: How Christianity Can Reach the West . . . Again* (Nashville: Abingdon Press, 2003) is, substantially, a book-length case study of how the Christian movement, launched by Saint Patrick's evangelization of Ireland, spread to many other peoples across the British Isles and to much of western Europe by indigenizing Christianity's forms to the specific peoples everywhere. Paul and Patrick invented indigenous Christianity many centuries before we even knew what to call it!

18. See Eugene Nida, *Customs and Cultures: Anthropology for Christian Missions* (Pasadena, Calif.: William Carey Library, 1975), and *Message and Mission: The Communication of the Christian Faith*, rev. ed. (Pasadena, Calif.: William Carey Library, 1990). See also Paul G. Hiebert, *Anthropological Reflections on Missiological Issues* (Grand Rapids: Baker Academic, 1994) and his *Transforming Worldviews*, cited above.

19. See David A. Seamands, *Healing for Damaged Emotions* (Wheaton, Ill.: Chariot Victor Publishing, 1981).

20. Robert C. Solomon's lecture series entitled *The Passions: Philosophy and the Intelligence of Emotions* (Chantilly, Va.: The Teaching Company, 2006) is a useful discussion of emotion theory, though his understanding of (and appreciation for) Christianity's contribution is thin.

21. Demasio, an influential scholar in neuropsychiatry, challenges the "Cartesian split" between reason and emotion in *Descartes' Error* (New York: Putnam, 1994).

22. George Campbell, *The Philosophy of Rhetoric*, edited by Lloyd F. Bitzer (Carbondale: Southern Illinois University Press, 1963), 77.

23. Jonathan Edwards, *A Faithful Narrative of the Surprising Work of God* (1737), in *A Jonathan Edwards Reader*, ed. John R. Smith, Harry S. Stout, and Kenneth P. Minkema (New Haven and London: Yale University Press, 1995), 65.

24. Ibid., 58.

25. Ibid., 60.

26. Ibid., 62.

27. Ibid., 63.

28. Ibid., 69, emphasis added.

29. Ibid, 71.

30. Ibid., 68.

31. Ibid., 71.

32. Ibid., 86.

33. Ibid., 76.

34. Ibid., 64.

35. Ibid., 85.

36. Ibid., 85-86.

37. Ibid., 86.

38. Jonathan Edwards, A Treatise Concerning Religious Affections, in A Jonathan Edwards Reader, ed. John R. Smith, Harry S. Stout, and Kenneth P. Minkema (New Haven and London: Yale University Press, 1995), 141.

39. Ibid., 144.

40. Ibid., 145.

41. Ibid., 147.

42. Ibid., 143.

43. Ibid., 143, 146.

44. Ibid., 149.

45. Ibid., 152.

46. Jonathan Edwards, The Religious Affections (Edinburgh: The Banner of Truth Trust, 1984 reprint), 266.

47. Ibid., 267; See 266-71 for Edwards's complete discussion of this point.

48. Ibid.,165.

49. See ibid., 164-71.

50. For Edwards's thorough reflection on spiritual power, see ibid., 153-64.

51. In this section, I am indebted to the work of Mark Lewis (whose dissertation I advised) in my summaries of the insights of several of the historical contributors to the theory of the sublime. See Mark William Lewis, "The Diffusion of Black Gospel Music in Postmodern Denmark: With Implications for Evangelization, Meaning Construction, and Christian Identity" (PhD diss., Asbury Theological Seminary, 2008).

52. Longinus, "On the Sublime," in Patricia Bizzell and Bruce Herzberg, The Rhetorical Tradition: Readings from Classical Times to the Present, Second Edition (Boston: Bedford/St. Martin's, 2001), 341-58.

53. Rudolf Otto, The Idea of the Holy: An Inquiry into the non-rational factor in the idea of the divine and its relation to the rational (New York: Oxford University Press, 1958), 1-40.

54. Ibid., 42.

55. Jean-Francois Lyotard, The Postmodern Condition: A Report on Knowledge (Minneapolis: University of Minnesota Press, 1984), 80-81.

56. See Michael Osborn's educational videotape I Have a Dream: The Nature of Great Speaking (San Luis Obispo, Calif.: Davidson Films, 1994). The following eight points are my summary of Osborn's lengthier discussion.

57. Ibid. I am quoting Osborn's quotation of lines from Longinus.

58. Ibid.

59. Ibid.

4. When We Reach Out, Whom Will We Reach?

1. No such pin map exists. I am simply using the image to dramatize my best estimates.

2. As this is being written, Charles Arn's Start a Heartbeat Ministry in Your Church is scheduled for publication in 2009. For churches that want to launch ministries for the groups of people they have a heart for, this book will take the place of the one we never had before.

3. Donald A. McGavran, Understanding Church Growth, 2nd ed. (Grand Rapids: Eerdmans, 1980), 245-48.

4. In this discussion, I am drawing especially from Eugene Nida, Message and Mission: The Communication of the Christian Faith, rev. ed. (Pasadena, Calif.: William Carey Library, 1990).

5. Michael Green, *Evangelism in the Early Church*, Revised Edition (Grand Rapids: Eerdmans, 2003), 363.

5. Evangelizing Pre-Christian People: A Thematic Perspective

1. Some churches elevate their "most spiritual" people to leadership roles. Spiritual devotion is, indeed, a prerequisite to *faithful* Christian leadership, but unless the church lives in an unchanging context, like a medieval village, it is never by itself sufficient for *effective* leadership. Some "saints" make disastrous leaders; they have learned to love God with their hearts, but not yet with their minds.

2. That rough evangelical consensus shifts some over time, but many leaders in recent history have usually agreed that the Christian faith should spread through public revivals or crusades; through tracts, billboards, or bumper stickers; through radio or television programs; through an Internet website; through the Roman Road or the four spiritual laws; or through some other formulaic approach to preaching to people one-on-one.

3. See Donald L. Miller and Tetsunao Yamamori, *Global Pentecostalism: The New Face of Christian Social Engagement* (Berkeley: University of California Press, 2007).

4. C. Peter Wagner, *Dominion! How Kingdom Action Can Change the World* (Grand Rapids: Chosen Press, 2008).

5. See, especially, the writings of Rodney Stark, such as *The Rise of Christianity* (Princeton: Princeton University Press, 1996); Roger Finke and Rodney Stark, *The Churching of America: 1776–2005: Winners And Losers In Our Religious Economy*, rev. ed. (New Brunswick, N.J.: Rutgers University Press, 2005); and Rodney Stark and Roger Finke, *Acts of Faith: Explaining the Human Side of Religion* (Berkeley: University of California Press, 2000).

6. See, especially, Lewis R. Rambo, *Understanding Religious Conversion* (New Haven: Yale University Press, 1995). Someone, one day, will read the literature on conversion and interview Christian converts in a range of churches and populations, and will write an influential text in "applied conversion studies."

7. Schaller has published more than forty books and has scattered his insights for informing congregational and denominational growth. Five books are most obviously related to expanding Christianity's ranks: *Growing Plans* (Nashville: Abingdon Press, 1983), *44 Ways to Increase Church Attendance* (Nashville: Abingdon Press, 1987), *44 Questions for Church Planters* (Nashville: Abingdon Press, 1991), *44 Steps Up Off the Plateau* (Nashville: Abingdon Press, 1993), and *A Mainline Turnaround: Strategies for Congregations and Denominations* (Nashville: Abingdon Press, 2005). Two books especially address major paradigm shifts that many churches need to experience: *The Seven-Day-a-Week Church* (Nashville: Abingdon Press, 1992) and *From Geography to Affinity* (Nashville: Abingdon Press, 2003).

8. In McGavran's last major book, he clarified that the years of field research were primarily to inform "effective evangelism." See Donald A. McGavran, *Effective Evangelism: A Theological Mandate* (Phillipsburg, N.J.: Presbyterian and Reformed Publishing Company, 1988). Nevertheless, the second edition of *Understanding Church Growth* (Grand Rapids: Eerdmans, 1980) remains his most comprehensive reflection. The 1990 third edition is essentially a condensed version of the second edition.

9. See George G. Hunter III, *The Celtic Way of Evangelism* (Nashville: Abingdon Press, 2000).

10. We know of at least one monastic community in the West that predated the Celtic movement—the community of Saint Martin of Tours. Martin launched the first mission to rural people in Europe. We believe that Patrick, then perhaps in his late twenties, once spent time at Tours and reflected his way toward a somewhat *different* approach to reaching the Irish.

11. Bede, *The Ecclesiastical History of the English People*, trans. Bertram Colgrave (Oxford and New York: Oxford University Press, 1969), 4.23.

12. See John Finney, *Finding Faith Today: How Does It Happen?* (London: British and Foreign Bible Society, 1992).

13. Hall introduced his then revolutionary idea that "culture is communication" in *The Silent Language* (Greenwich, CT: Fawcett Publications, 1959). *The Hidden Dimension* (Garden City, N.Y.: Doubleday, 1966) more thoroughly explored how humans communicate through space and, in *The Dance of Life* (Garden City, NY: Doubleday, 1983), through time. *Beyond Culture* (Garden City, N.Y.: Doubleday, 1976) is his most nuanced treatment of these themes. His autobiographical *Anthropology of Everyday Life* (New York: Anchor Books, 1994) reflects upon his experience in discovering other "primary message systems" within cultures.

14. See Dean M. Kelley, *Why Conservative Churches Are Growing* (New York: Harper & Row, 1972). Kelley reported that "strict" or "demanding" churches grow. In this writing, I have revised these insights to reflect how many of us within Kelley's tradition now characterize growing churches as "high-expectation churches."

15. The study interpreted by Win Arn, Charles Arn, and Carroll Nyquist, *Who Cares About Love?* (Arcadia, Calif.: Church Growth Press, 1986), reviewed questionnaire data from thousands of laypeople in hundreds of churches. The study demonstrated a compelling positive correlation between a church's growth and its people's perceptions of how loving and caring the church's people are toward one another, toward visitors, and toward the community outside the church. When they compared data by denomination, the dozen denominations that scored highest on the "loving-caring quotient" were all growing.

16. Some church leaders regard my chapter "Recovery Ministries as a Prototype for Outreach Ministries" as the best short introduction to addiction theory, the recovery movement, and recovery ministries. See George G. Hunter III, *Radical Outreach: The Recovery of Apostolic Ministry and Evangelism* (Nashville: Abingdon Press, 2003), 119-48.

17. To root your mind and soul deeply in the apostolic tradition, read Robert G. Tuttle, *The Story Of Evangelism: A History of the Witness to the Gospel* (Nashville: Abingdon Press, 2006).

18. For McGavran's first and most comprehensive reflection on the gospel's spread through social networks, see Donald A. McGavran, *The Bridges of God* (New York, NY: Friendship Press, 1955). McGavran's discovery has been replicated many times. "Diffusion" scholars have demonstrated, for instance, that presumably all innovations—such as new ideas, technologies, and products—spread across "diffusion networks." See Everett M. Rogers, *Diffusion of Innovations*, 5th ed. (New York, NY: Free Press, 2003), chapter 8. More recently, scholars have discovered that *happiness* spreads across social networks! Indeed, "happiness spread outward by three degrees, to the friends of friends of friends." See Maria Cheng, "Study Says Happiness Transfers from Person to Person," *Lexington Herald-Leader*, 5 December 2008, sec. A-3.

19. The book by Win and Charles Arn, *The Master's Plan for Making Disciples: Every Christian an Effective Witness through an Enabling Church*, 2nd ed. (Grand Rapids: Baker Books, 1998) is the most enduring approach to the ministry of evangelism based on Church Growth research and reflection.

20. See Miller and Yamamori, *Global Pentecostalism*, especially pages 22-25 and 197-99.

21. Willow Creek Community Church has taught converts, throughout the church's history, that the ministry of witness is central to Willow Creek's "Seven-step Strategy" for every member. Nevertheless, Willow Creek's recent self-study reported that their more mature converts are more likely to engage in witness than newer converts. See Greg L. Hawkins and Cally Parkinson, *Reveal: Where Are You?* (South Barrington, Ill.: Willow Creek Association, 2007). I would suggest that the main reason for this is that Willow Creek's model expects Christians to engage in the ministry of witness *alone*—on the job, at the health club, and so forth. Most new

converts, however, cannot (or feel they cannot) alone carry that much weight. In the following paragraphs I show how, in the Church Growth tradition, we recommend that mature Christians join new Christians in their outreach.

22. McGavran and I once identified these reasons in a lengthy conversation, each of us drawing from our interview data.

23. We lack the sufficient data to validate this claim. I offer it as a *very* conservative estimate.

24. For a more complete report on this research see George G. Hunter III, *To Spread the Power: Church Growth in the Wesleyan Spirit* (Nashville: Abingdon Press, 1987), chapter 4.

25. This reflection is consistent with Willow Creek Community Church's evangelism curriculum, which in the first lesson helps people discover that the presentation approach is *one of eight* approaches to faith-sharing we find modeled in the New Testament. See Bill Hybels and Mark Mittelberg, *Becoming a Contagious Christian* (Grand Raipds: Zondervan, 1994). I am suggesting, however, that the conversation model (which the *Contagious Christian* project did *not* feature) is the model *most* modeled and reflected in the New Testament, especially in the ministry of Jesus. (For verification, begin with John 4.) Furthermore, I am suggesting that most (if not all) Christians can engage in the ministry of conversation.

26. See chapter 3, "Christianity's Gospel and Its Ethic," in my book *Christian, Evangelical, & . . . Democrat?* (Nashville: Abingdon Press, 2006), for a more complete discussion of essential Christianity vis-à-vis the domesticated Christianity that many church people assume.

27. James Russell Hale, *The Unchurched: Who They Are and Why They Stay Away* (San Francisco: Harper & Row, 1980).

28. I should have reached this conclusion much sooner than I did. In the years when I was giving gospel presentations, when the receptors became people of initial faith it was *not* because the presentation accomplished that objective. Rather, my presentation raised questions in their minds, and they maneuvered me into conversation, usually multiple conversations over time, and it was the ministry of conversation that helped make the difference—especially when we included God in the conversation!

29. See Peter L. Berger and Thomas Luckmann, *The Social Construction of Reality: A Treatise in the Sociology of Knowledge* (London: Penguin, 1967). This understanding of conversion is spelled out in the second half of the book, which focuses on "secondary socialization."

30. Barbara Walters, *How to Talk with Practically Anybody about Practically Anything* (Garden City, N.Y.: Doubleday Books, 1983). As I recall, the word *with* was a major theme. We learn to talk with people, not to them.

31. Kerry Patterson, et al., *Crucial Conversations: Tools for Talking When Stakes Are High* (New York: McGraw-Hill, 2002).

32. Ibid., 3.

33. Richard Peace's *Holy Conversation: Talking about God in Everyday Life* (Downers Grove, Ill.: InterVarsity Press, 2006) is an excellent Christian source for preparing God's people for the ministry of conversion. It is designed in twelve sessions to prepare conversationalists, within groups, for Christ.

34. Mead was a philosopher and social psychologist at the University of Chicago. His foundational text was actually written, following his death, from the class notes of several of his students. First published in the early 1930s, the most available version is George Herbert Mead and Charles W. Morris, *Mind, Self, and Society: From the Standpoint of a Social Behaviorist* (Chicago: University of Chicago Press, 1967). Mead, son of a clergyman, probably would have liked the church taking his insights seriously!

35. For some analogous cases and inspiring reading, read some of the many published testimonies in the "big book" of Alcoholics Anonymous. These firsthand stories consistently feature

how the people used to talk to themselves when they were in the grip of addiction's mysterious power, and how they began talking to themselves differently, which helped lead to their recovery. See *Alcoholics Anonymous*, 4th ed. (New York: Alcoholics Anonymous World Services, 2001).

36. The five affirmations are always the same, but the phrasing varies.

37. Quoted in Stanley Ayling, *John Wesley* (Cleveland and New York: William Collins Publishers, 1979), 5.

38. John Wesley, "Minutes of Several Conversations," in *The Works of John Wesley*, ed. Samuel Jackson (Grand Rapids: Baker Book House, 1978), 8:303.

39. Vincent Donovan spent sixteen years as the Roman Catholic apostle to the Maasai people of east Africa. His *Christianity Rediscovered* (Chicago: Orbis Books, 1978) reflects, as in the title, how much he learned about Christianity's gospel and ethic from the experience of interpreting its meaning to a pre-Christian population of a very different tongue and culture from his own.

40. Quest's figure for "new Christians" includes people who had been nominal members of other churches (at least at one time) but had never been, by their own report, serious Christians. The church's data does not permit me to say, with precision, how many of these people represent "transfer growth" and how many represent "conversion growth." My interviews with new Christians at Quest would indicate that about half represent conversion growth; they'd had no prior church to transfer from. My sample, however, is not large enough to validate my "educated guess."

41. Quest Community Church is a member of the Willow Creek Association. That association has been remarkably influential in spreading the "seeker church" model. The three largest churches in Lexington are all members of the Willow Creek Association, and we observe a similar pattern in many cities. Chicago's Willow Creek Community Church was founded in 1975 as an "apostolic experiment," and I regard it as the most important apostolic experiment in my lifetime. I was, I am told, the first professor in theological education to interpret insights from the Willow Creek project to the wider church. My books, such as *How To Reach Secular People* (Nashville: Abingdon Press, 1992), *Church for the Unchurched* (Nashville: Abingdon Press, 1996), and *Radical Outreach*, introduced Willow Creek to many church leaders and, I am told, "legitimized" Willow Creek as a church "worth learning from." Willow Creek decided early to omit visual Christian symbols when they built their first facility. Innovative leaders do not get *every* decision right, and I have never heard or read a compelling argument for the omission of symbols. I suspect that Willow Creek's leaders bought, unreflectively, into the widespread but unspoken evangelical Protestant bias that the sense of *hearing* is the only sense that matters, and that *words* are the main, if not the only, medium of God's revelation. Although Protestants are not obligated to replicate Roman Catholic "smells and bells," I submit that all of the senses *do* matter, that multisensory communication is often more powerful than what can be achieved through hearing alone, and that the next pioneering churches may show us how to indigenize Christian symbols to the target population's aesthetic—as we have already learned to do with their favored genres of music. In virtually every other major mission field on the planet, we have already learned how to develop indigenous expressions of Christian symbols.

6. Evangelizing Pre-Christian People: A Narrative Perspective

1. George G. Hunter III, *How to Reach Secular People* (Nashville: Abingdon Press, 1992).

2. George G. Hunter III, *Church for the Unchurched* (Nashville: Abingdon Press, 1996).

3. George G. Hunter III, *Radical Outreach: The Recovery of Apostolic Ministry and Evangelism* (Nashville: Abingdon Press, 2003).

4. Since in early twentieth-century British English the word *strange* meant something like *complex* in American English today, I have substituted *complex* for *strange* in his statement.

5. Once, while I was leading a seminar for circuit-riding pastors in the outback of New South Wales, Australia, a pastor said, "Mr. Hunter, I hear you like cats. I wish you could meet my cat. She is really unusual. She has eighteen legs." I was astonished, "You have an eighteen-legged cat?" "Yep," he replied, "figure it out for yourself. She's got two forelegs—two fours are eight. She's got two hind legs—that's ten. She's got two on each side—that's fourteen. She's got one in each corner—that's eighteen legs!" I had to do some math before I discovered the simplicity on the other side of his complexity.

6. Let me anticipate the reader's question: Yes, in the ministries and social networks of the church's people, *much* takes place beyond the pastor's range of awareness; the pastor might even be oblivious to much that goes on. This is to be desired. For instance, in a sixteen-hundred-member church, in which perhaps four hundred members are engaged in outreach and average reaching at least one new person per year, the pastor should *hope* that there is more going on that he or she is directing or monitoring!

7. While some of the following points are transparent in the book of Ruth, others may only be implied. Nevertheless, when we know that some factors are true of all or most converts, we can infer them from Ruth's case on more slender evidence.

8. Many Christians, of course, still have something like a one-link chain in mind! Readers who reflect upon chapter 5 and this chapter will understand why evangelism, when it is done, is done badly more often than almost anything else people do.

9. See Charles G. Finney, *Lectures on Revivals of Religion*, ed. William G. McLoughin (Cambridge, Mass.: Harvard University Press, 1960), chapter 10.

10. See Joel M. Charon, *Symbolic Interactionism: An Introduction, an Interpretation, an Integration*, 9th ed. (Upper Saddle River, N.J.: Pearson Education, 2007), especially chapter 6.

11. Helmut Thielicke, *The Trouble with the Church: A Call for Renewal* (New York: Harper & Row, 1965).

12. The most enduring and influential delineation of this social reality is Peter L. Berger and Thomas Luckmann, *The Social Construction of Reality: A Treatise in the Sociology of Knowledge* (Garden City, N.Y.: Doubleday, 1966).

13. Bishop John Finney led a comprehensive study of British converts to Christianity in the 1990s. His *Recovering the Past: Celtic and Roman Mission* (London: Darton, Longman & Todd, 1996) was, to my knowledge, the first study to demonstrate this trend. I later contributed to this discussion in *The Celtic Way of Evangelism: How Christianity Can Reach the West . . . Again* (Nashville: Abingdon Press, 2000). Of all the conclusions we have reached from historical and field research in evangelization, this is the most difficult conclusion for most Christian leaders (Protestants *and* Catholics, especially those stuck in modernity) to agree with. Their inherited paradigm virtually decrees that people must believe *before* they can be accepted into the fellowship.

7. Leading the Change from Tradition to Mission

1. In *Radical Outreach: The Recovery of Apostolic Ministry and Evangelism* (Nashville: Abingdon Press, 2003), "Old East Side Church" became my fictional name for the two hundred thousand American churches that still expect next year will be 1957.

2. Those occasional "converts" in traditional churches often were once active members of another church in an earlier period of their lives, but they dropped out (perhaps when they moved to another community) and did not then join another church. In time, their former church removed them from its membership roll. Now, as they join Old East Side years later,

their former church no longer counts them as members and therefore cannot send a transfer letter, so Old East Side classifies them as "new Christians." So most of the very occasional "converts" more precisely represent restoration growth. Furthermore, other occasional "converts" have married church members and later joined their spouse's church. Old East Side's actual impact upon card-carrying pagans with no prior church involvement or relational attachment is less than negligible.

3. See Wallace Fisher, *From Tradition to Mission* (Nashville: Abingdon Press, 1965).

4. See the following books, all published by Abingdon Press: *The Contagious Congregation* (1979), *Church Growth: Strategies That Work* (with Donald McGavran, 1980), *To Spread the Power: Church Growth in the Wesleyan Spirit* (1987), *How to Reach Secular People* (1992), *Church for the Unchurched* (1996), *The Celtic Way of Evangelism* (2000), *Leading and Managing a Growing Church* (2003), *Radical Outreach: The Recovery of Apostolic Ministry and Evangelism* (2003), and *Christian, Evangelical and . . . Democrat?* (2006).

5. My project, which commends an apostolic paradigm for the churches, has closer kinship with movements and books that have championed seeker churches, purpose-driven churches, high-expectation churches, and missional churches, and with the books of Donald McGavran and Lyle Schaller in the Church Growth tradition that reflects from field research, than with many of the other approaches mentioned in this paragraph.

6. Hunter, *Leading and Managing a Growing Church*, 23-24.

7. Ibid., 22-23.

8. See James Collins and Jerry Porras, *Built to Last: Successful Habits of Visionary Companies* (New York: HarperBusiness, 1994).

9. The watershed book was Terrence E. Deal and Allan A. Kennedy's *Corporate Cultures* (Reading, Mass.: Addison-Wesley, 1982). Successive editions of Edgar A. Schein's *Organizational Culture and Leadership* (San Francisco: Jossey-Bass, 1985, 1991, 2004) have helped a generation of leaders exegete their organization's culture and identify new ways to lead and manage.

10. Many thinkers and writers moved toward this perspective more or less concurrently. One early, authoritative, and influential source was Daniel Katz and Robert L. Kahn, *The Social Psychology of Organizations* (New York: Wiley, 1966).

11. One can find apparent exceptions—churches that can show you a plan, but the church is not growing. You invariably find, upon examination, that the plan was not informed by any good analysis of the church or the community, or many of the people never understood the plan or bought into the plan, or the written plan sits in a file drawer, but the leaders do not refer to it when making decisions.

12. Chris Lowney, *Heroic Leadership: Best Practices from a 450-Year-Old Company That Changed the World* (Chicago: Loyola Press, 2003), 8.

13. See George Keller, *Academic Strategy: The Management Revolution in American Higher Education* (Baltimore: The Johns Hopkins University Press, 1983).

14. George Keller, *Transforming a College: The Story of a Little-known College's Strategic Climb to National Distinction* (Baltimore: The Johns Hopkins University Press, 2004).

15. Hunter, *Leading and Managing a Growing Church*, 63-64.

16. I think there are compelling reasons to side with the leaders who modify the "attainable" criterion to read "attainable *with stretch*." The point is that goals need to stretch the church beyond what it has already been achieving, and even beyond what it could do with a higher priority but within its own strength; the goal should be large enough that the church would have to rely on the Holy Spirit to attain it.

There is, however, a contrasting point that is virtually as important. Set a goal that, with God's help, you could *exceed*. Churches that have exceeded last year's goals have more momentum than churches that fell short—even if the first group set lower goals and the second group achieved more.

17. I have developed this strategic principle, which only represents a recovery of the apostolic genius of early Christianity, in two books. *The Celtic Way of Evangelism* explains how the ancient Celtic Christian movement, begun with Patrick's evangelization of much of Ireland, reached the "barbarian" populations of Europe, providing strategic clues for reaching the "new barbarians" found in all of our cities today. *Radical Outreach* develops this same theme throughout much of church history and shows how this radical apostolic principle is often applied today.

18. See *Radical Outreach*, chapter 5, for a recent and rather thorough discussion of addiction, its known causes, what we have learned about helping people get into recovery, and the recovery movement's apostolic potential for many churches.

19. Almost no field of study has attained unanimity on any complex issue, and this includes strategic planning. Henry Mintzberg has long feared that strategic planning may give insufficient attention to vision and may rely too much on mere plans; he is the leading name in management that prefers some other way. In what Christian writers purport to be in the church's service, more than one "authority" has debunked strategic planning. The latest is Will Mancini. His *Church Unique: How Missional Leaders Cast Vision, Capture Culture, and Create Movement* (San Francisco: Jossey-Bass, 2008) announces "the fall of strategic planning," but it reflects from *no* authoritative sources in strategic planning literature. Another chapter dismisses Church Growth. Although it lists some book titles, many are not Church Growth books in (or near) the McGavran tradition, and the chapter reflects no insight from sources that are. Elsewhere, *Church Unique* features the importance of "culture"—but draws from no authoritative sources. It commends a kingdom of God focus for churches, but misrepresents Jesus' good news of the in-breaking "reign of God"; and the book *vastly* exaggerates the extent to which churches are dissimilar from one another. The writer is an imaginative stylist but, like so many books that publishers are grinding out, it is more sizzle than steak.

20. Schaffer wrote many articles on the approach, but his wisdom is summed up in *The Breakthrough Strategy: Using Short-term Successes to Build the High Performance Organization* (New York: Harper & Row, 1988). I devoted chapter 10 of *Leading and Managing a Growing Church* to an expanded discussion of this strategic approach, including a range of local church case studies.

21. Schaffer, *The Breakthrough Strategy*, 4.

22. George Odiorne, *Management and the Activity Trap* (Nashville: Harper & Row, 1974).

23. Jennifer Hewlett, "Ducky Ending: Babies Were Trapped, No Mom in Sight," *The Lexington Herald Leader*, 13 June 2008, sec. A, pp. 1, 6.

INDEX